MEMOIRS

OF

A WORKING MAN.

"IF I ONE SOUL IMPROVE, I HAVE NOT LIVED IN VAIN."

LONDON:
CHARLES KNIGHT & Co., LUDGATE STREET.

1845.

London: Printed by WILLIAM CLOWES and SONS, Stamford Street.

PREFACE.

During the last ten or twelve years, I have often thought of writing some account of myself, but was deterred from doing so by various and, at the time, insurmountable obstacles. Having, however, about four years ago, mentioned my wishes to several friends on whose judgment I could safely depend, they advised me to undertake the task. Thus encouraged, I went to work, and, at length, have brought it to a conclusion.

As some apology for the imperfections which will, doubtless, be manifest to the judicious reader, I have to say, that the manuscript was written at uncertain intervals, under many literary disadvantages, and in the midst of various difficulties, among which that of much bodily disorder and weakness must be specially noted.

Should what I have thus committed to paper be at all amusing or instructive to the reader, I shall not have wholly misapplied my labour.

INTRODUCTION.

BY THE EDITOR OF THE WEEKLY VOLUME.

The celebrated Gibbon, in the introductory portion of his own 'Memoirs,' speaking of the autobiographies of various men of letters, says—" Such portraits are often the most interesting, and sometimes the only interesting part of their writings; and, *if they be sincere*, we seldom complain of the minuteness or prolixity of their personal memorials." This, no doubt, is perfectly true with regard to the self-executed portraits of men of any literary eminence. But shall we feel an equal interest in the "personal memorials" of a man of humble station, unknown to the world—who may, indeed, have had as strong aspirations after knowledge as the most illustrious author of his age, as

INTRODUCTION.

much satisfaction in its acquirement, but who has walked through life humbly and obscurely—who has laboured with his own hands to earn his daily bread—who has endured the bitterest poverty—who has been prostrated, for years, by chronic sickness—whose earliest lot was toil and indigence—and whose accumulations for the days when the small rewards of toil shall be no more are of the very scantiest amount? Such a man is the 'Working Man' whose 'Memoirs' are now presented to the reader. We believe that these 'Memoirs,' in their own degree, will interest as much as any other of the kind which deal not with striking adventures, but present a clear reflection of the mind of the writer, which is sincere. Gibbon truly says—" The public are always curious to know the men who have left behind them any image of their minds. . . . . The student of *every class* may derive a lesson or an example from *the lives most similar to his own.*" When Gibbon wrote his 'Memoirs,' it was scarcely present to his view that *every class of students* would be a term of far wider application half a century after his own day than when the love of books was a rare distinction. One of his contemporaries wrote the life of a *Staymaker*, who had made himself a competent Greek scholar, and was a wonder in those times. same age produced its usual share of prodigies the shape of rhymesters who had never been to school, who were patronized as foils to the rhymesters who had been to school. But such examples indicated nothing of the tendencies of a class. Had a *Tailor* written his Memoirs, who had nothing to record of marvellous adventure, nothing of precocious talent—who had never been patronized out of the proper performance of his duties—who had only to show how the humblest lot is not incompatible with literary tastes, with the love of the excellent, with cheerful thoughts reflected from the contemplation of nature, with tranquil musings derived from a familiarity with nature's best interpreters, and, above all, with a contented spirit founded upon deep and constant piety—if such a person had appeared with his 'Memoirs,' half a century ago, how utter would have been his neglect! Contempt would have been too much honour for him. But the circle is widened. He has now *his own class of students* to sympathise with him, and to cherish his lessons and examples.

The peculiar interest of these 'Memoirs of a Working Man' is in the view which they present the mode in which the mind of the writer has been formed, under the most adverse circumstances. He makes no claim to any extraordinary powers of understanding; he displays no unwonted energies. He is neither the " village Hampden," nor the "mute inglorious Milton," whose "destiny obscure" was determined by his lot in life. Yet of him, as of many others *now*, who have " kept the noiseless tenour of their way," it *cannot* be said that

> " Knowledge to their eyes her ample page
> Rich with the spoils of time did ne'er unroll."

That page has been unrolled to many an eye, in the midst of " chill penury ;" and yet " the genial current of the soul" has not been frozen. This, we believe, is a distinction which has only begun to be understood in our own day. It is not to be inferred that a man who diligently performs all the duties of the humblest calling is necessarily ignorant; or that if he reach some of the acquirements which were once held to belong to the noble, the wealthy, and the professionally learned, he must be discontented with his station, and become incapable of performing the offices by which he claims a share of the labour-fund, which is the only inheritance of him and of his class. It is beginning to be felt that knowledge is the common property of the human family—the only property that can be equally divided without injury to the general stock. These 'Memoirs of a Working Man' were written, I believe, without the view of inculcating this principle; but one of my chief inducements to include them in this series is to add another to the few public examples of the blessings that directly, and independent of any collateral advantage, belong to the cultivation of a taste for reading and composition, amongst the great body of our fellow-men who pursue the most mechanical and laborious employments of society. The lesson to be taught by this little book is the same that was taught by 'Mind amongst the Spindles,'—namely, "that a strict and diligent performance of daily duties is no impediment to the exercise of those faculties, and the gratification of those tastes, which, whatever the world may have thought, can no longer be held to be limited by station."

The author of these 'Memoirs' has not published them with his name. Nor does he mention the names of any persons with whom he has been brought into contact; nor even of the two or three very creditable little works which he has previously published. There can be no objection, however, for me to mention that he is the author of one of a series called 'The Guide to Trade,' published by Charles Knight and Co., and that in 1840 he was introduced to me by a gentleman well known in the world of letters and of art, as a highly deserving man carrying on a little business for himself as a tailor, with a dependent family, and struggling with the severest ill health. The Manual for the Apprentices to Tailors, which he then wrote, gave abundant proof of his technical skill. But this treatise also exhibited the rational and contented tone of mind with which the writer looked upon his own vocation in life. After offering some sound practical advice on the subject of morals and religion, he thus concludes:—" If he [the apprentice] attends to these admonitions and counsels, he will ultimately find that, although he may not be able to command great wealth, or fame, or station, he will both acquire and enjoy what is far better than all these together—namely, good health, a peaceful and contented mind, a fair reputation, and in general as much money as will enable him to procure all the necessaries and many of the comforts of life. And should he at any subsequent time be enabled to become a master, he will be all the more likely to succeed well in that capacity, for having been an industrious, careful, and well-behaved journeyman. Such cases are by no means rare; and although all cannot be masters, much less wealthy masters, yet all may be worthy and intelligent men, and, being such, may reasonably look for a sufficient maintenance, and also for much real and lasting enjoyment."

Holding in respect the principles and character of this good man, I was gratified when he asked me to look over the 'Memoirs,' which he had been preparing for several years. His wish was to publish them by subscription. In their original form they were incomplete, as far as regarded the period of his life to which they came down; and they were somewhat too diffuse in particulars which could only be interesting to himself and his family. I recommended him to continue them with brevity to the present time; to curtail such matters as most retained the quality of "garrulous old age," of which tendency he was quite aware; but on no account to suppress what would be interesting to all—the history of the formation of his habits of thought, and thence of his system of conduct—the development of his intellectual and moral life. Upon receiving the Manuscript thus altered and completed, I proposed to publish it in the Weekly Volume. This is the extent of my editorial duty. I have not added, nor have I altered, a single word. The purity of its style is one of the most remarkable characteristics of this little book.

CHARLES KNIGHT.

January 17, 1845.

MEMOIRS

OF

A WORKING MAN.

CHAPTER I.

WITHIN a hundred miles of London there is a large and pleasantly situated town, which is remarkable for its antiquity, and also for its having been the scene of some important historical events. It is moreover, worthy of notice on account of the many remains of buildings and other works of ancient art which still exist within its boundaries, as also in its immediate neighbourhood.

The town is said to have been founded by a colony of Romans, and further to have been one of the earliest of the Roman settlements in Britain.

There I was born, but neither of my parents were native inhabitants. My mother came hither from a small town nearly twenty miles distant, and my father from the remoter part of a neighbouring county.

Of my ancestors I know nothing, but from the family surnames I infer that they were poor persons. The surname of those on my father's side was evidently taken from the occupation of him who first bore it, and denotes that he was a vassal of the class. Those on my mother's side seem to have been of equally humble origin, as the surname appears to have been suggested by sun-burnt or weather-beaten complexion.

Whether any of their descendants, on either side, ever emerged from their native obscurity and poverty, I cannot tell; but in the absence of all traditionary evidence on this head, I conclude that they did not. An event so gratifying to human vanity as that of a family rising from a lowly state to one of comparative wealth or high station, would not be likely to fall into oblivion.

I am the more confirmed in this view because both my father and mother were the children of poor parents; my grandfather on the one side having been a husbandman, and on the other a journeyman wool-comber. My father followed the occupation of a husbandman until he was of mature age, when he became what may be called "man of all work" to a wine-merchant. My mother lived as servant in the same family, and from this circumstance followed the acquaintance which subsequently led to their marriage. Soon after this event my father became cellar-man to his master, and was in comfortable circumstances. He seems to have then been both a useful servant and a good husband. My mother was a worthy woman, and a good housewife—careful, orderly, and industrious. For several years they lived together comfortably; but subsequently lost all their advantages by my father's imprudence. Unhappily he contracted a habit of drinking intemperately, which ultimately became together with every article of her household furniture, were kept in the cleanest possible condition. She carried her dislike to dirtiness so far as to request every person coming into her house to be careful not to soil, or otherwise put out of order, the well-scrubbed and "neatly sanded floor." I was not disposed to be of either slovenly or dirty habits, and therefore seldom if ever gave her any trouble on these accounts. She did not allow me to be idle, but alternately employed me in helping to knit stockings and in reading. While I was unemployed I found a never-failing source of amusement in scanning the grotesque figures and scenes delineated upon the Dutch tiles with which the chimney-corners were covered and decorated. I believe that these pictures, rude as they were, helped me a little the better to understand what I read to her out of the Bible and other religious books. I believe that these readings were rather useful to me than otherwise; but this, perhaps, arose partly from the pains she took to indulge my fancy in other matters, and partly also from the motherly way in which she endeavoured to make me understand what I read.

As a general rule, I think it may be fairly determined that the requiring children or youths to read a given portion of the Sacred Scriptures, at a prescribed time, as a lesson or task, is very injudicious. It is yet more so, I think, when it is required of them to commit whole chapters or even paragraphs to memory.

I remember to have read of Lord Bolingbroke, that he attributed his distaste for theological truth to the circumstance of his having been obliged when a child to read frequently, and for a considerable time at each sitting, out of some book on divinity. For myself I remember to have had a somewhat similar feeling in regard to two chapters in the New Testament, one of which my father appointed as a task for me, and the other for one of my brothers. I could not for many years regard these chapters with the same satisfaction as I could all the other parts of the sacred writings.

About this time I also gained the good-will of an aged woman who sold cakes, sweetmeats, and fruit, and was moreover a dealer in little books. With her, as with my aunt, I was quite at my ease, as she freely gave me much that tickled the palate, and also allowed me ample scope for amusing my childish fancy. I had even then a taste for reading, which was here gratified by my being permitted to read all the little stories which she kept on sale. They were, in truth, childish trifles; but I still think of them with pleasure, because they were associated in my case with many pleasant recollections. Were I to follow the impulse of my feelings, I should here give their titles and some account of their contents, but I must forbear trifling to that extent. Here also I met with some books of a higher order; but which were then far beyond my comprehension. Among these were 'Hervey's Meditations,' 'The Pilgrim's Progress,' and an illustrated (?) Bible. This last work was crowded with engravings, which were called embellishments. Each of these was pompously dedicated to some great personage, and was evidently thought by the publisher, to be no small ornament to the book. I much suspect, however, that they would cut a poor figure by the side of the engravings in any similar work of the present day. They were, I think, sorry affairs in regard to both design and execution. As to the designing part, some of them were not a little ludicrous. I well remember being much amused with the oddness of several, but will mention only two. In the first the artist intended to give an illustration of the passage (in St. Matthew's Gospel) which speaks of a man attempting to pull a "mote" out of his "brother's eye," while a "beam" is in his "own eye." This was represented by the figures of two men, one of whom was depicted as having a small splinter of wood sticking in his eye, and the other as in the act of attempting to pull it out, although a fair-sized beam was protruding from his own. In the second engraving an attempt was made to illustrate St. Paul's being miraculously restored to sight; and here the artist represented the Apostle as having a pair of balances in the act of falling from his eyes. But I am wandering, and must retrace my steps. When at home I was usually employed in some useful way; for although I was still very young, yet I had learned to assist in household work, to knit stockings, and to do several other things. My mother saw the importance of training me early to habits of industry and good order. She thought it no argument against my doing anything, that it was usually performed by girls; nor would she at all excuse me from doing it upon this ground. I must have begun to learn at a very early age, for I have no recollection of the time when I could not knit or assist in other household business; nor do I remember the time when I could not read with tolerable ease and correctness. My eldest brother taught me to write, and it must have been when I was very young, for I cannot recollect when I first began to use a pen.

I was allowed but little time for play, perhaps not enough for the preservation or improvement of my health and cheerfulness, nor was I ever allowed to play in the streets. But I fully acquit my parents of all blame herein. If they erred, their error was on the right side; for no acquisitions of physical health or of animal spirits can compensate the *man* for the injury done him when a *child* by having been then allowed to contract habits of idleness or dissipation. As to playing in the streets, I am fully convinced that it is a practice from which much lasting evil is pretty sure to accrue; I am, therefore, grateful to my parents for having kept me from so baneful an indulgence, and have always prohibited it in the case of my own children. Yet this necessary precaution on the part of the parents is almost sure to be the occasion of much inconvenience to their children. It was so in my case, and it has been the same in my own family.

There is a remarkable antipathy on the part of street-playing children against such as are not so, who in general may be easily known by their being less dirty, ragged, or disorderly than are those who are accustomed to roam about the public ways.

The principal source of this hostility is, I think, Envy; for there is much of the "Dog in the Manger" temper among the indolent, the dirty, and the dissolute poor. They will not take the trouble to secure the advantages arising from industrious, cleanly, and sober habits; and they would fain prevent all others from gaining them. But as they cannot do this, they frequently do all they can to make their more prudent and reputable neighbours as uncomfortable as it may be possible to make them. They will therefore call them by opprobrious names; charge them with being imitators of the dress or the manners of the rich; and, moreover, will often go out of their own way and take much pains in order to insult or to injure them.

Whether I am right or wrong in ascribing this hostile feeling and conduct to the cause above stated, I know not, nor does it much signify. The fact remains the same; for it is certain that the children of the orderly and decent class of poor people are in many cases persecuted by those of the opposite class, both as fiercely and relentlessly as is a domesticated bird or quadruped when it falls in the way of the untamed and more powerful of its species.

For several years I suffered much from this maltreatment, which I certainly never provoked, for I loved peace, and, moreover, had neither strength nor courage enough to warrant my being the aggressor. Yet I was often insulted—and sometimes injured—not only by children of my own size or age, but also by such as were both much bigger and older than myself; and in some instances, by adult persons. I, at length, dreaded going into the streets unprotected, as much as some children would have dreaded a severe correction.

In stating these matters I am perhaps running the risk of trifling; yet, as it often happens that—in regard to their bearing and consequences—even "little things are great to little men," so in my case these seemingly trivial matters had an important use. They served to enforce what I had been taught concerning the wickedness of doing wrong to others; while they inspired me with a thorough hatred of oppression, injustice, and cruelty. My natural timidity would not allow me to join in any game that involved either danger or much difficulty; while, in consequence of my feeble constitution, I could not engage in any active amusement without being both speedily and painfully fatigued. To these circumstances I may perhaps attribute a part of my early indifference to many of the pastimes that usually are so attractive to children. I soon learned to regard even harmless pleasures as not being "worth the pains" of the chace, or of the weariness and other inconveniences by which, in my case, they were always followed. It was thus, I think, that I contracted an early taste for retired habits and quiet amusements; a taste which has accompanied me all through life, and which has, I believe, been the means of preserving me from many evils, while it has been the instrument of adding very much to my comfort and well-being.

My favourite amusements were reading, gardening,*

* Or rather, playing at gardening, for my ground was so circumscribed that all its stock and produce were little more than would have sufficed for the use of his Lilliputian majesty. But I always loved flowers, and I had some, even in this

and walking in the adjacent fields and meadows. Of these, however, reading was my chief delight; for I could avail myself of this the most easily and regularly. I willingly left every other pastime for the sake of a book that suited my taste. And I valued this pleasure the more, because it was only at leisure times that I was permitted to enjoy it. I had not much time at my own disposal, being usually employed in one or other of the ways I have already stated. If it were at knitting, I was forbidden to read until I had finished my allotted task. Sometimes when I tried to evade this law, I was detected, and severely reprimanded by my mother, whose maxim was, that two distinct things could not both be well done at the same time. At other times I succeeded in gratifying my wishes by getting into some secluded place, where I could avoid observation. In order that I might the better escape detection, I took pains to get through my task in due time, and, moreover, was careful to do it well. In these efforts I was generally successful, for, on making the experiment, I found it possible to knit—both quickly and neatly—without having much occasion to look at my work. In this way I beguiled many a tedious hour at the time I am now referring to, and also during several years following, towards the close of which I thus contrived to read 'Robinson Crusoe,'

---

diminutive spot: I valued these the higher, because they were my own, and, moreover, of my own raising. Let not the reader smile when I tell him that my collection was made up chiefly of some heart's-ease, primroses, and common marigolds, with a little mint, and a few slips of southernwood.

and a brief 'History of England,' with some other books whose titles I do not now remember. The books that first fell in my way, besides those that belonged to my parents, were few, and of little worth. At that time the stock of books within the reach of poor children was very small, while the price of such as were useful was generally higher than poor people could afford. There were then no cheap well-printed neatly bound books on subjects at once instructive and amusing, such as are now so abundantly supplied by benevolent societies and enterprising publishers. The once general prejudice against educating the poor was then very prevalent, while many of the poor had no wish to be taught. Moreover, the books that were given to them were generally printed badly, and done up in unsightly covers; while their contents were seldom much more attractive than was their external appearance. It did not in those days seem to be understood that abstract treatises on religious or other serious subjects were not adapted to fix the attention of children and other young persons. There was but little recognition of the obvious fact that the human mind needs recreation as well as instruction; that it desires amusement, and, therefore, will seek to obtain it from frivolous, if not dangerous sources, in the absence of such as are useful and innocent.

The importance of combining amusement with instruction in books intended for the use of little children, was not then sufficiently estimated; although the fact itself could not be unknown by all observing and reflecting persons. The surprising tenacity with which the memory retains whatever has been learned in childhood, naturally suggests the necessity of taking care that what is then acquired should be worthy of remembrance. For myself, I have now—after an interval of more than forty-five years—a clear recollection of the little books which I read when a child, and which then formed the principal part of a poor child's " Entertaining Library." I can remember all about them, their titles, their contents—and their external appearance. Some, being without covers, were sold for the price indicated in the following laudatory stanza, with which, and a suitable vignette, the title-page of one was embellished:—

> "A very pretty thing
> For daddy's darling;
> Tom Thumb and the piper
> And all for a farthing."

Others were of higher pretensions and prouder aspect, being enclosed in gay covers of party-coloured or gilded paper, and therefore were sold at the comparatively large price of a halfpenny.

It may seem to be little better than trifling to write about farthing or halfpenny histories of 'Tom Thumb,' 'Jack the Giant-killer,' 'Little Red Riding-hood,' and the like; but when it is considered that the human mind generally retains, in mature years, much of the tastes and habits it acquired in childhood, it will not be difficult to believe that important consequences may and often do arise out of circumstances or practices which in themselves are of little worth or moment.

From much observation, I am led to think that the

preference shown by many persons for such books as treat of wholly fictitious or merely frivolous subjects, to the utter neglect of all such as are instructive and important, is in a great degree owing to their having been, while children, accustomed to read very little besides fabulous and foolish tales. That this perverted or false taste has an injurious bearing upon their habits and condition, is, I think, too evident to need any laboured proof. In my own case, such books as these did me but little harm, inasmuch as my prevailing desire was to obtain some useful knowledge; consequently I was soon satiated with what was adapted only to please a vagrant or a sickly fancy. When I first began to read for amusement, I had, as has been hinted, access to but few books that were likely to be useful as well as entertaining. My parent's stock consisted of two Bibles, a Common Prayer Book, a Universal 'Spelling-book,' Watts's 'Divine and Moral Songs,' with some tattered and odd volumes of sermons and other theological disquisitions. Among the latter of these was nearly the whole of a huge folio volume, which was then as much beyond my power to handle conveniently as its contents were above my comprehension; yet, in the absence of more attractive compositions, I sometimes read considerable portions of even this giant-sized and uninviting volume. But my attention was chiefly given to the historical and poetical parts of the Bible; these I read with great interest, but mingled of course with much childish wonder and misapprehension. How much I needed the aid of a competent teacher will be manifest when I state that, for a long time, I believed the books of "the Kings" and of "the Chronicles" to be unconnected narratives of two distinct series of events; and also, that the four Gospels were consecutive portions of the history of Jesus Christ, so that I supposed there had been four crucifixions, four resurrections, and the like. I was, indeed, sometimes perplexed by the apparently repeated occurrence of events so nearly resembling each other; nor could I perceive the exact design or bearing of these events; but I knew no one of whom I could ask for the needed explanations.

I was greatly interested with the biographical notices of the patriarchs—among which the history of Joseph and his brethren* attracted my particular attention; but in regard to these also I needed the assistance of a competent expositor and casuist, to illustrate what seemed obscure and to explain what appeared to be wrong in their characters and conduct. I was also much gratified by reading the book of Job, the Psalms, the book of Ecclesiastes, and some of the prophetical books of the Old Testament. The won-

---

* This narrative was an especial favourite with my mother also, as I believe it is with all among whom the native power of perceiving what is beautiful is not encumbered with any artificial theories. The singular beauty of this simple story is, however, acknowledged by all descriptions of readers. I have somewhere read that even Voltaire, that most artificial and sophisticated specimen of human nature, gave his opinion in its favour, saying, "I meet with no tale among the Eastern fictions comparable to this; in almost every part it is of admirable beauty; and the conclusion draws forth tears of tenderness. It is more pathetic than Homer's 'Odyssey,' as a forgiving hero is more moving than he that gluts his vengeance."

derful events foretold in the latter excited my admiration, and sometimes a more grave emotion. I was either much surprised, or elevated, or filled with awe, according as I perused the more wonderful, or beautiful, or sublime portions of these unrivalled compositions; although I had but little if any knowledge of their real import. The book of the Revelations inspired me with similar feelings. Of course I understood its wonderful narratives and descriptions according to the literal import of the language employed; and therefore my imagination was more powerfully affected than it would have been, had I known it to be highly if not entirely figurative.

The merely preceptive and the doctrinal parts of the Scriptures did not engage much of my attention until my thirteenth or fourteenth year; yet I had read the greater part of them long before that time, and remember to have been much affected by several detached passages—especially by that on the resurrection of the dead contained in the First Epistle to the Corinthians.

But I was the most pleased with the poetry of the Bible, and of this I much preferred such parts as are illustrated by imagery drawn from natural scenes and objects; for, as soon as I was capable of observation, I was powerfully affected by natural beauty and sublimity. The magnificent scenery of the visible heavens—both by day and night—filled me with pleasing wonder; and I was equally delighted, although in a different manner, with the multitudinous and ever varying beauties of the earth. Each of the seasons was to me beautiful and therefore a source of pleasurable emotions: these, however, were different in the different seasons; that is, each season produced its peculiar and appropriate feelings. I well remember with what indescribable pleasure I contemplated the return of spring, and how gladly I hailed every indication of its near approach. The early flowers, the first butterfly, the renewed song of birds, the milder temperature of the atmosphere, with the increased splendour and warmth of the sun—all these were to me sources of heart-felt "delight and joy." And I hailed the harbingers of the other seasons with no less enthusiasm. I rejoiced to see the full-grown foliage, the tall grass just ready for the mower's scythe, the young of various animals approaching to maturity, with the numerous other objects that betoken the approach of summer. I was, perhaps, yet more glad to see the forerunners of autumn, as this was my favourite season; partly, I think, because its mild and equal temperature was then, as it now is, grateful to my external senses, but chiefly because of its being the time when the anxious hopes of the spring and summer months are usually exchanged for fruition. Nor was the approach of winter unwelcome, for it was with pleasure rather than with uneasiness that I looked at the fading face of nature, or listened to the voice of the rude wind, or contemplated the other impressive phenomena that precede its advent.

I am no longer susceptible of these lively feelings, yet I am not indifferent to the objects which once excited and nourished them. There are, indeed, moments when I look back with regret upon the time when I could not contemplate nature, whether in its lovelier or its sublimer aspects, without having these emotions awakened to a degree that was sometimes almost painful, because I had no means of giving them utterance. I was a timid, shy, sensitive boy, one whose outward nature alone was associated with surrounding persons and objects. The mind and the heart were in solitude. I knew no one to whom I could unveil the thoughts that perplexed the one, or tell of the feelings which frequently oppressed the other. Thus situated, what remained for me but to seek some other medium of giving expression to my speculations and emotions? I did this, and almost unconsciously fell upon the expedient which is, as it would seem, natural to man—I mean, the composition of verse. I well remember my first effort in this direction, when I contrived to string together some twelve or sixteen lines. These were, beyond doubt, sufficiently childish; but, notwithstanding their puerility, I have often wished I had preserved them, merely as a record of the force and tendency of my early emotions. With this temperament of mind, it was natural that I should be much gratified on discovering that the Bible would much help me in giving utterance to feelings which, but for its aid, could then find no adequate medium of expression.

At this time I knew but little of the doctrines propounded in the Bible; I had, however, a somewhat better knowledge of its moral precepts, and could in some degree enter into the spirit of its devotional parts. What I thus learned was, I think, much enforced by the perusal of that well-known little book Watts's 'Divine and Moral Songs,' which I read with so much interest as to impress them indelibly upon the memory. From these sources, in connection with such oral instruction as I received, I learned something concerning the first principles of Religious Truth. The amount of knowledge gained was indeed small; yet it was of much use as a means of qualifying me to learn more readily, in afterlife, much that I wished to know upon this weighty subject.

Until my ninth year I had learned little or nothing of any merely human science, but my ignorance herein was involuntary, for I had no means of commanding the sources of knowledge. A series of Pinnock's Catechisms, or of any other simple elementary treatises, would at that time have been a treasure of no small value; but such helps as these were not then in existence.

As a necessary consequence of my unfavourable circumstances, my notions were for the most part not a little childish; so much so, indeed, that they did not always satisfy myself. I had in truth many misgivings as to their correctness, on account of the difficulties or contradictions which they seemed to involve. Thus, for example, I supposed the sky to be a solid surface of a blue colour, with a great many bright spots upon it, of which the sun and moon, as being the largest, naturally attracted my especial attention. I of course supposed the sun to be no larger than its apparent size seemed to indicate; yet I could not comprehend how so small an object should communicate so much light and heat as I perceived it did. Neither could I understand why or how it was that the moon should give light without heat; and I was equally at a loss to account for its frequent changes of form, as also for its periodical disappearance.

As to the causes that produce the succession of the seasons, I neither had nor could obtain any information about them that seemed to be either satisfactory or probable.

Nor was I better able to ascertain the causes or the nature of many atmospheric phenomena: this, however, I had the less cause to regret, because I was pleased rather than alarmed by storms of thunder, lightning, or wind, unless they were more than usually severe; but, had I known anything of their immediate causes, or of their real nature, this pleasure would have been much diminished. As it was, I had full scope for the play of my childish imagination, whose conjectures, wild and strange as they indeed were, gave me far higher gratification than perhaps I could have derived from a more rational source.

As to the interchange of day and night, I readily conjectured—what I afterwards learned had been taught by eminent philosophers—that it was caused by the revolution of the heavens around the earth. But as I supposed the latter to be only a vast plain, united to the sky at the horizon, I was utterly at a loss to reconcile my theory concerning the motion of the heavens with the notions I held respecting the form and position of the earth. Besides these difficulties there were others equally knotty, and which defied all my efforts to surmount them; for I wished to know the thickness of the earth, what it was that supported it, and what was underneath that supporter, and so on : thus my young mind was bewildered, and sometimes vexed or wearied, while it found no way of escape from the labyrinth in which it was entangled.

Nor was I more happy in my attempts to learn something about the great divisions of the earth's surface. I sometimes heard persons talking about America, the East and West Indies, France, Ireland, and other countries, but as to their situation or any other particular I could get no satisfactory account.

There was also a good deal said about the continental countries of Europe, but as they were collectively called " the Continent," without any distinctive appellation either to mark what continent was intended, or what part was meant of the continent referred to, I of course took the phrase to mean a separate and distinct country, like England; but none could tell me whether it was so or not, nor whether it was in Europe, Africa, or America. As to Asia, I do not remember to have known that it existed, at any rate under that name, until I learned it from books; nor until then did I know the distinction between a continent and an island, nor, indeed, whether there was any difference between them.

I also heard much talk about the American war, the French revolution, the Irish rebellion, and other public events; but it was all of the most vague and hearsay character, so that I was but little the wiser for what I heard. Moreover, as regarded the topography or the history of my own country, I was equally at a loss for the means of getting instruction. I knew neither its position, extent, nor divisions, nor more than a very few of either its natural or its artificial productions. Of its metropolis I heard just enough to excite my wonder, so that for a long time I had not a few extravagant notions respecting its size, wealth, and curiosities. I know not that I heard even the name of any other considerable or remarkable town in England, except that of one which everybody called "Brummagem," and this seemed to owe its celebrity to its being, as was asserted, the place where base copper money was made. The good people of this town have had many and grievous sins laid to their charge, of which I charitably hope they neither were nor are guilty.

I just knew that there was a king and a queen, a Prince of Wales, judges, bishops, dukes, lords, and the like, and I also understood that there were two houses of parliament, but as to their respective powers, privileges, or functions, I knew nothing; nor was I much more enlightened upon the subject of corporate or municipal rights and immunities, for I well remember being unable to comprehend what was meant when asked whether my father was free of the borough in which we resided.

Of chronology, viewed as a science, I learned no more than I did of other sciences; nor do I now remember either when or how it was that I first got any correct notion respecting dates. The first incident concerning these that I recollect, is the difficulty I felt in comprehending why the date of 1798, which I had been accustomed to use in my writing-book, should suddenly be altered into 1799. When this in its turn gave way, and I was told to write that of

1800, I think my difficulty was about the same. By the time that 1801 came in, I think I had got some notion why these changes were made. Thus slowly and irregularly did I acquire most of what little I learned in my earlier years.

In short, with the exception of a little knowledge of the first principles of religion, and of the duties connected with the domestic life of poor people, I continued almost without teaching during a great part of the time in which appropriate instruction is so important to a child, especially to one whose youthful years are destined to be spent in learning to work. This, however, was not through any neglect on the part of my parents, since neither of them had been so far instructed as to be able to teach others: what they did know they readily communicated, and this, although small in amount, always had a useful tendency.

My thoughts at this period sometimes turned upon myself, and then I encountered new difficulties. With a natural, although childish curiosity, I wished to know from whence I came. It seemed strange that I could not remember coming into existence, as, in like manner, I often wondered why I could not remember the moment of falling asleep, although I had made many efforts to that effect. I perceived that I was a living and conscious being, surrounded by other beings of the same kind, placed, without any effort or consent of mine, in a world of whose surface I knew little more than the spot occupied by the town in which I lived. I had, indeed, been taught that *this* world, with all its productions and its inhabitants, was made by God; and, moreover, could read for myself the Bible history of the creation and of the primitive condition of man, yet I was not hereby fully satisfied. There were many things that I wished to know, upon which both the Bible and my other instructors were silent. I did not suspect that some of these matters were not necessary to be known, nor that others were beyond the reach of human knowledge, or I might perhaps have avoided taking much useless and sometimes vexatious trouble.

I could form some notion of the manner in which the first man was made, but could not comprehend how I could have been formed by the same being as he was, because I had learned just enough of human history to know that none besides the first parents of mankind were formed by the immediate and sole agency of the Deity. The constitution of my nature also perplexed me. I had been told I was a creature compounded of body and soul. The one I could see and form some notion of, and this more than sufficiently tasked my powers, for I could not comprehend the mysteries connected with its structure and motions. But the other I could not see, except in its effects, and I often wished to know something about its origin, its birth, and its constitution, together with the nature and extent of its powers, and the manner of their operation. My wishes were, however, as fruitless as were my speculations, and of these I may truly say that

"—— they found no end, in wandering mazes lost."

As to its future existence in a state of happiness or

misery, this was a subject which sometimes occupied my thoughts in a very grave manner; and although these musings were doubtless alloyed by many childish and erroneous fancies, they yet had a salutary influence upon my affections and conduct.

CHAPTER II.

I OUGHT before to have observed that when I was about five or six years old my mother began to keep a dame's school. This obviated the necessity of sending me to a similar school. I became one of her pupils, and was much pleased with my school-fellows. I also gained some profit as well as pleasure by their coming under my mother's care, being thereby enabled to peruse several small books belonging to the children, which otherwise would not have come in my way. I thus gathered some additional knowledge, which, although not equal to my wishes, was nevertheless useful, as it helped to enlarge my range of thought and to prepare me for ampler instruction at a future time.

Among these books was a brief abstract of that amusing story 'Robinson Crusoe,' which I read with much eagerness and satisfaction. I only regretted its brevity, for I became so deeply interested in the fortunes of its hero and of his man Friday, that I would fain have read a full account of their adventures. This, however, was a gratification reserved for a future time. Another book which thus came in my way was Mrs. Barbauld's 'Hymns for Children,' which I soon perceived to be exactly suited both to my taste and my capacity. Here I met with descriptions of rural scenery, life, and manners, which delighted and instructed me. The perusal of these simple yet admirable compositions served to heighten the satisfaction with which I even then contemplated the beauty or the grandeur of nature; I perceived that they enabled me to discover new sources of mental pleasure, and moreover to express my emotions in an intelligent and appropriate manner. With these in my hand I remember to have walked in the neighbouring fields and meadows, and to have contemplated the surrounding scenery with great delight. More than forty years have since elapsed, in the course of which I have read much of the best poetry, yet I still remember these unpretending little pieces with undiminished pleasure; while there are moments in my experience when I would willingly exchange the gratification of reading nobler compositions for the pleasurable emotions with which I first perused these beautiful hymns.

Perhaps I value them at too high a rate, but hope to be excused herein, when I state that I was indebted to them not only for much innocent and delightful amusement, but also for some important moral lessons. I therefore look back on them with something resembling the affection and veneration with which one regards an old and valued friend. I must not conclude this notice without heartily commending them to the best attention of the juvenile reader; they are admirably adapted to improve both the mind and the heart. It was about this time that I first met with Milton's 'Paradise Lost,' in a thick volume with engravings and copious notes, probably a copy of Bishop Newton's edition of that noble poem. I found it, however, to be little better than "a sealed book." Its versification puzzled me, while the loftiness of its subjects confused my understanding. I went on much in the way I have been describing, until I was nine and a half years old, when I was sent to school, and thus began what I may call a new era in my history. Before, however, I enter upon this, I will notice two events, which I omitted to mention in their proper places.

The first is the great scarcity of wheat and other bread-corn during the year 1800.* This to poor people was the source of much distress, in which of course I participated. My father's wages were but ten shillings and sixpence per week, and my mother's little school brought from two to three shillings more. With very little besides this scanty income, they had to provide for the wants of themselves and four children, while bread was sold at the enormous price of one shilling and tenpence for the quartern loaf. We were consequently forced to put up with very insufficient fare, and sometimes with that which was rather hurtful than nutritious. Potatoes also were excessively dear, and moreover were of bad quality through the wetness of the preceding summer. A quarter of a peck of these, which cost fourpence, with a little

* This was caused by a very unpropitious harvest-season. I well remember having seen large breadths of corn, which had been cut down, but could not be housed because of the heavy and almost incessant rain. This had been exposed to the wet, yet warm weather, until the grain had sprouted from the ears, to the length of several inches. I was just old enough to know that the consequences would probably be very distressing to poor people.

melted suet poured over them, and a very small allowance of bread, constituted the dinner of five out of the six persons in the family. The sixth was too young to be able to eat solid food. No white bread was allowed to be made in the town, nor was the bread made permitted to be sold until it had been out of the oven twenty-four hours. These and other regulations were intended to diminish the consumption of wheaten flour. The privations of the poor would have been much more severe, but for the generous and Christian-like sympathy of their wealthier neighbours, who distributed three times in each week, during several consecutive months, large quantities of rice, with good soup and other necessary articles. Of these we had the full share to which our numbers entitled us, and this made an important addition to our otherwise meagre fare. I take pleasure in recording my unfeigned gratitude to the benevolent donors. I now turn from a subject which in itself is unpleasing, to one of a more inviting character.

This refers to the public rejoicings in the town on account of the general peace of 1802. I was much amused with the novel spectacles I then witnessed. The town was generally illuminated; the streets were filled with people; the church-bells were ringing; bonfires were blazing; and everybody seemed to be happy. For myself, I could almost wish again to be a child, if thereby I could once more feel the light-heartedness which these festivities produced. But there was a subject connected indeed with these rejoicings, but of far greater importance, especially to such as had endured privations through the recent scarcity. This was the great and numerous benefits that were expected to arise from the return of general tranquillity. "Peace and Plenty" was the motto to many a device exhibited at the illuminations. This had already become the general watchword, and everybody seemed to expect that their hopes of general and lasting prosperity would soon begin to be realised. In these cheering anticipations I most heartily joined, little suspecting that they were so soon to be cut off by the return of war. Of this unpropitious event I must now forbear to write, as it is time to give some account of myself while under the care of a schoolmaster.

The school to which I have referred was supported by a congregation of Protestant Dissenters. It consisted of twenty-five boys, who were taught the elements of reading, writing, and arithmetic. They were also partly clothed at the expense of the subscribers. The period for which the boys were admitted was three years. The vacancies in the school were filled up at the close of the year, and it was required of the applicants for admission that they should be able to read in the New Testament to the satisfaction of the managing committee. This regulation involved an ordeal which to me was a rather formidable affair. I dreaded it so much the more because, as I knew but little of its nature or extent, my imagination was at liberty to draw a rather fearful picture. I well remember the subdued feelings with which I wended my way to the place of trial. It was on a winter's evening, when the dreary aspect of everything around me was in keeping with the solemnity of the business in which I was engaged. It was well for me that my good mother took me under her wing, as otherwise I should certainly have been confounded when I came before my examiners.

These worthy but to me awful personages were assembled in a large upper room of an ancient inn. They were seated around a fire that was blazing cheerfully, and almost eclipsing the light of the candles, which of themselves would have but just sufficed to make "darkness visible." I was too much abashed to allow of my surveying the room very closely; what I saw of it, therefore, was only by occasional and hasty glances. I observed, however, that the table was well furnished with bottles and glasses, pipes and tobacco, indicating that the company present thought it wise to relieve the cares of business by a little of that which tends to make the heart glad.

I cannot now remember all who were present, but have a clear recollection of several, among whom was the minister of the congregation; an aged, venerable looking man, whose close-fitting, neatly curled wig, and somewhat antiquated dress, accorded well with his age and character. There was also a worthy gentleman, one of the deacons, whose portly figure, powdered head, and commanding aspect filled me with profound awe. He was, however, a kind-hearted and affable man. I could have spoken without much perturbation to either of these good men, had I met him alone and casually; but to see them all at once in a strange place, and invested with authority to question me, was too much for one so timid as I then was. A novitiate monk in the august presence of His Holiness and a full conclave of Cardinals, or a presumed heretic at the tribunal of the Inquisition, could hardly feel more discomposed than I did when directed to read aloud in the hearing of my assembled judges. I obeyed this dread mandate with much trepidation, but was enabled to do it so as to escape censure. My mother gave such further information about me as was required: upon which I was unanimously elected, with some expressions of approbation.

Thus ended my much dreaded trial, to my no small relief and satisfaction; I had passed through the ordeal unscathed, although much frightened, and I could not but rejoice at my success.

I was well satisfied with the treatment I had met with from my examiners, but, as a faithful chronicler, I am bound to state that I was not a little puzzled at a part of their proceedings. They were smoking; and as I had been accustomed to regard this practice as indicative of intemperate or loose habits, I was greatly surprised at seeing "grave and reverend" men like these wielding the ominous tobacco-pipe. Even the minister was thus employed;—this was the most inexplicable circumstance of all: I afterwards learned that he was an inveterate smoker, which intelligence further increased my perplexity. I feared that all was not right, but I was too poor a casuist to grapple with so knotty a question; I was therefore compelled to leave it until I should be more equal to the task.

I went home, however, in good spirits, for I anticipated both advantage and pleasure from this change in my circumstances; nor was I, as the sequel will show, at all disappointed in my expectations. In due time I went to the school-room, where I soon got the better of my natural timidity, at least so far as to feel prepared for the proper performance of my duties. The school-room was large enough to have accommodated a hundred and twenty boys; it had, therefore, a somewhat deserted and dreary aspect, especially in winter-time, when the boys were glad to get near the fire, which was liberally provided for their comfort. The windows of the room opened upon a spacious and well-stocked market-garden and nursery-ground. It commanded a rather extensive prospect of the country beyond it. This was to me a very gratifying circumstance, particularly during the fine weather, and I accordingly took some trouble to secure a seat close to one of these windows. In this I soon succeeded, and thereby added considerably to my means of enjoyment. I yet remember with pleasure the many happy hours I spent in sitting apart from the other boys—in whose frolics and tricks I took but little interest—and, while gazing upon the scenes before me, almost losing myself in vague yet delightful anticipations of the happiness which I then hoped to realize even in this life. This, however, has proved to be but a waking dream; yet was it a dream so delightful, that I could wish to have it repeated, although at the certain expense of a similar disappointment.

But I must leave these speculations, and return to my narrative. Here I must briefly notice my two schoolmasters, for there were two, although the school was so small. This arrangement, however, was for the convenience and at the expense of the elder master, whose other avocations frequently called him from home. He was a very worthy man, having moreover considerable talent, with much literary and scientific knowledge; being, however, of a modest, unpretending disposition, and perhaps not fully conscious of his powers, he made no effort to ascend

"The steep where Fame's proud temple shines afar."

Yet I cannot help thinking that a man who could invent a "Theory of Comets," measure lances with St. Pierre, and write well upon the science of "Sacred Music," ought not to have spent the whole of his long, virtuous, and useful life in a state of comparative obscurity.

He took no part in teaching the boys, nor did he often come into the school-room, so that I should have known but little of him except for the following circumstances:—Among his other acquirements he had learned the art of surveying land and buildings: being esteemed as an able, worthy man, he was much employed in measuring estates, within a circle of about twenty miles from his residence. As he wanted some one to draw the measuring-chain, and to do other little things which a boy could easily perform, he sought for a helper among the boys in the school, when, to my great delight, his choice fell upon myself.

By this arrangement I soon had opportunities of seeing a little of the adjacent country, of which until then I was almost wholly ignorant. I had never yet been more than four miles from the town, and was very imperfectly acquainted with its outskirts. Except a few of the fields and meadows close to our dwelling, nearly every other place was as new to me as would have been a foreign country. It was, therefore, quite natural that I should think much of the pleasure to which I was so unexpectedly introduced; nor will it seem strange that I should then consider a journey of fifteen or twenty miles from home as a long one. I will not deny that I eventually regarded myself, in comparison with my compeers, as a traveller rather out of the common order; for I could boast of having seen several market-towns, a considerable number of villages and hamlets, many gentlemen's seats, and a yet greater number of farm-houses. In each of these objects there was something new, and therefore pleasing to an observant, inquisitive boy. Our journeys were made in various directions, so that I had opportunities of seeing many new prospects. Some of these I saw more than once, and at different seasons of the year; I therefore viewed them under different aspects. The greater number were doubtless without much beauty, but some of them I still consider to have been worthy of my admiration.

I was also much gratified by the kindness with which I was in general treated by the farmers and others, at whose houses we took up our abode while measuring their lands. In some of these I witnessed much of the true old English hospitality to visitors, together with much of that friendly social intercourse which once so generally prevailed between the farmer and his servants. Many a time have I been served at one meal with more victuals than was needful for a day to a boy of my age and habits; and in these cases I have been not a little embarrassed, being about equally afraid of displeasing my generous host if I left any orts upon my plate, and of suffering considerable inconvenience if I ate the whole of my allowance. My confusion was not a little increased if I fancied that I was noticed while thus hesitating between what I thought was due to good manners, and what I owed to my personal ease and comfort. Sometimes I was compelled to sacrifice the former, and in one instance was glad that I had the courage so to do, for the good-natured farmer made me easy by letting me perceive that he had helped me so liberally in order to try my ability at the knife and fork. When the grounds were large, and there were more than an ordinary number of difficulties in the way of working quick, it was necessary to employ three or four days in measuring the estate. In these cases, when we happened to be quartered in a house of the old-fashioned sort, our sojourn was very pleasant to myself, and I could perceive that it was far from being unpleasant to my worthy master. I remember one of these instances with peculiar satisfaction, because everything bore the aspect of comfort and good feeling; master, mistress, children, servants, and guests, all sat at the same table, partook freely of the same food, and joined, if they pleased, in the same conversation. In the evenings the scene was to me especially agreeable, for then the labours of the day were done, and the whole household was assembled round a huge fire made upon the hearth the only fires that quite suit either my taste or convenience; there was a spacious and most convenient chimney-corner on each side of the fire, in one of which I sat, much pleased with the novelty of the whole scene, and well satisfied with the good and substantial fare with which I was freely supplied. I slept in the men-servants' room—a dark but warm and comfortable place—where I was happier with my rather unyielding bed of flocks, and my coverlet of new horse-cloth, overlaid with clean, sweet-smelling sacks, than, I dare to say, many a monarch is with all the luxurious accommodations and indulgences of a palace.

A little before this time I had been reading that entertaining little volume, Miss Taylor's 'Original Poems for Children,' one of which, "The Truant Boys," had particularly gained my attention, and I had partly committed it to memory. While at work on the farm, we had to measure some meadows intersected by a small river, on which, at no great distance, was a water-mill. The scenery so nearly resembled that described in the little poem referred to, as to bring it fully upon my mind, and I have not yet forgotten a line, after an interval of more than thirty-seven years, during which I have lost the recollection of numberless matters far more weighty. I name this trifling incident as a further example of the great importance of putting into the hands of children such compositions only as may be remembered with safety and advantage in future years.

But I must not enlarge further upon these little matters: suffice it to say that my master was a kind-hearted, considerate man. He always treated me more as a son than as a servant; permitting me, when we lodged at an inn, and where consequently he bore the charges, to eat and drink of the same fare and to sit at the same table or fireside as he did. He would, moreover, sometimes tell me of such little things respecting the neighbourhood we were in as he thought likely to instruct or amuse a boy like myself.

On one of our journeys he had occasion to attend the county assizes, which were then being held in a town not far from where his other business had called him: here I saw what was to me truly a novel spectacle; the crowds of people thronging the streets that led to the courts of law and justice—the costume of the barristers, who were bustling to and fro, and whom I mistook for judges—the numerous constables and other guardians of the public peace, together with the magnificence, as I thought it, of the public buildings, all conspired to fill me with admiration. There was but one part of the whole scene which affected me painfully, and that was the files of prisoners, with fetters upon their legs and chained together like beasts of burden, proceeding from the gaol to the criminal court. I had never before seen human nature in so degraded a state, and the sight gave me a feeling of pain which not all its novelty could remove.

My good old master continued to employ me while I remained in the school, and also afterwards, until, a desirable opportunity offering for my learning a trade, I could no longer serve him: he, notwithstanding, continued to notice me in his usual kind manner, and I was glad whenever I came in his way, for I had much reason to regard him with gratitude, respect, and veneration.

He followed his usual avocations until the infirmities of age came upon him and rendered him incapable of further exertion, when he found a quiet and respectable asylum in one of a number of almshouses which a benevolent man of the preceding age had built and liberally endowed for the benefit of aged and decayed tradesmen. Here, as throughout his long and industrious application to business and study, he pursued "the noiseless tenor of his way," until, his earthly course being ended, he was called to a nobler and a happier state of being.

I take pleasure in thinking about him, and sometimes can almost fancy I see his venerable-looking form, his kind and gentle aspect, his simple yet becoming attire, his somewhat curious gait and manner, for he had a habit of almost continually shaking his head and shrugging his shoulders; and I can almost imagine that I yet hear his shrill voice running over, as was his usual practice, some sacred melody, which gave a happy intimation of his mental tranquillity and enjoyment.

My other schoolmaster was altogether a different kind of person: he was a good penman, tolerably skilful in arithmetic, and generally attentive to his duties. His proper occupation was that of a shoemaker, and he was accustomed to fill up his spare time, during school-hours, by making or mending shoes. Unhappily he was too fond of strong drink, and was often more than half intoxicated, but contrived to conceal this from the other master. When he was in this state he was very ill-tempered, and was guilty of administering undeserved correction: he did this, moreover, with much severity and indiscretion. I yet retain a clear recollection of his having, when half inebriated, severely punished me with a heavy leather strap upon the palms of my hands. The occasion of this punishment was a very trifling one: I had written as an exercise the word "hyperbole;" on showing him my writing, he proceeded to flog me in the way I have described, and that too without telling me where or how I had done wrong. I felt at the time that I was very unfairly treated, and I still think that I might have been far more mildly corrected even had I been blameable.

This incident made an indelible impression upon my mind, and produced one or two rather curious effects in regard to my association of ideas; during many years from that time I felt an invincible dislike to the luckless word which had been the innocent occasion of my sufferings. Even to this day I am reminded of them whenever I deliberately use this word. Nor is this all, for it were no *hyperbole* to affirm that the formidable leather strap " in gorgon terrors clad " is still occasionally brought to my remembrance, especially when I see a similar weapon. But though I have not forgotten the punishment, I have long ago forgiven my master, of whom, except in this instance, I had no cause to complain. My chief reason for noticing his faults is that I may by this example show the necessity there is that all who have the care of young people should be able to govern themselves: any deficiency here will be very unlikely to escape the notice of their pupils, who will soon learn to despise such as are wanting in self-respect. The consequences which naturally follow from this state of things are too obvious to need pointing out.

My master took pains to teach me, and the more so because he saw that I was willing to be taught. I was, indeed, resolved to learn all I could, and therefore was not satisfied with merely getting through my allotted tasks, but voluntarily went beyond them, especially in arithmetic. Whenever I was unable to get on without assistance, I asked, and always obtained, my master's help: by these means I eventually became superior to my schoolfellows in regard to writing and figures, and as I was also tolerably clever at orthography and reading, I was promoted to the first seat on the first form, thus becoming what was called "head boy." I naturally considered this to be a station of considerable dignity, and now suspect that I failed to bear it "so meekly" as I might have done, for I soon perceived symptoms of ill-will in some of my compeers, which probably was provoked as much by my own imprudence as by their envy at my success; yet if I was proud of my superiority, I certainly was not selfish, for I freely helped any boy who requested it: sometimes, indeed, I did this at the risk of displeasing my master. I remember his once getting behind me when I was thus engaged, in order that he might see to what extent I was giving help; it so happened that I was only giving some general directions, or I should probably have again felt the weight of the leather strap, and perhaps rather severely, as my master would have been smarting from a sharp blow on the face which he received by my suddenly throwing my head backwards while he was looking over my shoulder.

Once in each week we were required to commit to memory a rather large portion of 'The Assembly's Catechism:' this for a time gave me some trouble, which put me upon making several experiments in order to see whether I could not lessen it. After a failure or two, I hit upon a plan which fully answered my purpose: the time for repeating this lesson was Saturday morning, and as I wished to have all possible opportunity for reading what was then more entertaining than a catechism, I wanted to defer studying it as long as might be prudent: my plan was to leave it until Friday afternoon, when after getting through my other business I sat down to this, and read it over again and again until I had got a general idea of the whole; I then exercised myself by trying to repeat it from memory, referring to my book only when I was at a loss. This I continued to do at short intervals until bed-time, when I read it over, and afterwards repeated it as well as I could until I fell asleep. On the following morning I invariably found that I could go through it both readily and correctly, so that I had no further trouble about this part of my duties.

In general I could easily get through my afternoon's work in less than an hour, while the usual time for being in the schoolroom was three hours. I thus had full two hours of spare time, which I continued to spend very pleasantly, and perhaps usefully: my main object was indeed amusement, but the recreation I chose was, I think, instructive also; this was reading, for which I had now greater facilities than formerly. I borrowed such books as I could from my schoolfellows, but sometimes found this to be an unsatisfactory plan: on one occasion I wished to read a book, which, however, the owner would not let me have without a pecuniary consideration; I therefore hired it for a stipulated time, but shortly after I had paid him, which was at the time of hiring, he reclaimed it, and refused to return the money: I was indignant at his injustice, but there was no remedy, for he was strong enough to enforce the law of "might" against that of "right," and therefore I quietly submitted, although I was sorely grieved at being hindered from using 'The Looking-glass for the Mind,' and the more so because I had hired the book at the expense of all my cash, amounting to no less a sum than three halfpence.

This incident taught me to be more circumspect in making bargains with schoolfellows, by none of whom was I afterwards thus defrauded, either of pence or pleasure.

My ill-success in borrowing of the boys served to strengthen my purpose of applying to my master. On my asking him he readily granted my request, nor did he ever revoke his grant: the books were chiefly old and odd volumes of the 'Arminian' and the 'Gentleman's' Magazines; these, though of but little intrinsic value, were to me a treasure, as they helped to give me a wider and more varied view of many things than I had previously been able to command. I perused them very much in the way of those undiscriminating readers who devour

"The total grist unsifted, husks and all."

Yet as there was nothing deleterious in the aliment, its somewhat heterogeneous character was perhaps rather beneficial to my mental constitution than otherwise, in like manner as bread made from unsifted meal in some cases more suitable to the stomach than that which is composed wholly of finer flour. I was then desirous of knowing a little upon a variety of subjects, and the miscellaneous contents of a magazine were well adapted to meet both my wishes and my wants. Perhaps it was partly owing to my perusing these volumes in the way I did that I contracted that omnivorous, perhaps morbid, appetite in regard to reading, which, not seldom, I have endeavoured to appease by very uncouth or uninviting fare; such, for example, as treatises upon law or medicine. I once had recourse to a dish of *anatomical* reading, and actually got through the whole, consisting of four large volumes. I thus contrived to draw refreshment, if not nutrition, from very unpromising sources, during several years. There was, indeed, hardly any species of literary composition from which I could not manage to get some amusement, if not instruction; and although from prudential motives I have long ceased to read in this indiscriminate manner, I yet retain a strong inclination to look through the whole of every book or paper that comes in my way, and have no doubt that I should, were time allowed me, daily go through the entire mass of advertisements, as well as all the other contents, of that mammoth among newspapers, a double 'Times.'

I continued to go on in the way I have described during the remainder of my school-going time. In plain writing and also in arithmetic I acquitted myself respectably: as to reading aloud I was able to get on tolerably well, but wanted to be taught something more of pronunciation and emphasis; these, however, were matters to which the master gave but little attention, so that I learned almost nothing about them while I continued at school.

In after years I endeavoured to supply this defect, not however by the aid of a professed teacher, but by observing the way in which public speakers of reputation pronounced the words respecting which I needed instruction. I also derived much assistance herein from reading poetry, as I here found it necessary to observe how certain words required to be spoken in order to preserve the measure or harmony of the composition.

Of grammar neither myself nor my schoolfellows were taught anything, except to repeat by rote the brief grammatical exercises contained in the 'Universal Spelling-book;' but, as the master gave no explanation of these, either as to their nature or use, they were nearly if not quite unintelligible to his pupils. For myself, I could not comprehend why we were made to spend time, which I could have used much more pleasantly, about what seemed to be quite as useless as it was uninteresting. I have since then thought that the master was himself ignorant of grammar, and that his only motive for giving us all this extra work was that he might keep us employed. If he had apprised me of the great utility of grammatical knowledge, I think I should have made an effort to acquire it; but as I heard nothing upon this head, I regarded the whole subject as being unimportant, while some of its parts, such as the declension of nouns and the conjugation of verbs, seemed to be little better than mere nonsense.

I thus remained wholly ignorant of the construction of my native tongue, until the proper time for being instructed therein was gone by; for, although in after years I endeavoured to learn a little upon this subject, I made but small progress, as both my hands and head were then fully employed upon more imperative matters. The result has been, that I have continued to this day a mere novice in regard to this important branch of knowledge.

We were allowed two holidays in the year, each of three weeks' duration, one at Christmas, and the other in the harvest-time. The latter was given in order that we might have opportunity for gleaning corn in the adjacent fields. This, however, my parents would not allow their children to do, being of opinion that there was no *real* advantage accruing from it, except where people had no other employment. I do not now regret that I was otherwise employed during these holidays, although at the time I should perhaps have preferred gleaning before knitting stockings, which was my usual work when away from school. If, however, I had been allowed to choose betwixt having or not having holidays, I should have decided for the latter, as I was more willing to be at school than is usual with young people.

I have already stated that the scholars were partly clothed. This clothing consisted of coats, breeches, and caps; the two first named being made of green baize with bright metal buttons, and the last of green worsted, with a scarlet-coloured tassel and band. When I put on these clothes for the first time, I am free to confess that my hitherto slumbering vanity suddenly started up and inspired me with rather lofty notions concerning my personal appearance. I clearly remember the pleasurable feeling with which I then set out for school, arrayed in my best trim, with a nosegay fixed in a button-hole of my coat, while I doubted not that my dress was as much admired by others as it was by myself. But these gratifying thoughts and pleasant feelings were very short-lived; as I soon perceived that I was neither a happier nor a more important personage than before. Thus ended my pride of dress, for I have never since been able to derive pleasure from this source, and can account for the generally prevailing vanity of grown persons, in regard to apparel, only upon the principle expressed by the poet, that

"Men are but children of a larger growth."

CHAPTER III.

I have before hinted that when I was at home I had but little time for amusement. But what leisure I could command was spent pleasantly enough in either reading or gardening. I found much pleasure in the latter pursuit, and, therefore, spared no pains to bring my little plot of ground into a good condition. My father was a rather clever practical gardener, although he knew but little of scientific gardening. But he was fond of the occupation, and would rise with the sun, during even the longest summer days, in order that he might have time to tend his flowers and culinary plants before he went to his daily labour, to which he set out at five o'clock. In the evenings he was generally employed in a similar manner.

By means of much good management, his garden became what I then thought to be a beautiful spot, and I still think it to have been creditable to my father's industry and skill.

He usually contrived to have a good stock of cucumber-plants, which he tended with especial care, and was in general very successful, the produce being both large and of a fine quality.

He also took much interest in the cultivation of flowers. He had not indeed many different kinds, but what he had were generally healthy and beautiful specimens of their respective species.

In the management of my own miniature garden I thus had the benefit of my father's example, of which I availed myself to the best of my ability. I accordingly stocked my ground with as many flower-roots and plants as it could well hold; and subsequently had the pleasure of seeing them turn out well. I was particularly gratified when I could exhibit a small yet perfect specimen of

" ——the prickly and green-coated gourd."

In keeping my garden free from weeds I was exceedingly particular, as I was also to prevent its soil from forming itself into clods. But out of this latter niceness arose an evil which I had not foreseen; for as the soil was rather heavy, it would, soon after being watered, form itself into a hard unbroken crust, which was quite as unsightly as were the clods, and moreover quite as difficult to put right.

Among my other gardening exploits I must not omit to mention that of raising several kinds of herbs, such as mint, thyme, rosemary, and southernwood, from slips or cuttings placed in bottles of water, until they formed roots large enough to allow of their being put into the ground. Let not the reader smile at my ignorance or simplicity when I state that I then regarded this method of raising herbs as a discovery of my own. I certainly did thus regard it, and with some reason, for I knew nothing concerning it, until I perceived that a cutting of southernwood which I had thus put into a phial was throwing out a profusion of roots, at which I was both surprised and elated. As I turned my discovery to a practical use, I found less difficulty than before in raising such herbs as are propagated by cuttings.

There were some other amusements to which also I was inclined, and of which I will give a brief account, trusting to the reader's forbearance while I act the child a little longer. Among these was one which was supplied by a community of ants whose place of abode was in a crevice at the top of an old wall that bounded my father's garden. Hither I often resorted to watch the movements of these very curious insects. I was much amused with their seemingly intelligent methods of proceeding with their work. The regularity with which they closed the entrance to their habitation in the evening, and opened it in the morning, was to me a curious fact, as also was that of their shutting it up just before rain, and opening it soon after the rain ceased. I was much surprised at the rapidity and completeness with which these operations were effected, and equally so at the good order which they maintained both in these and other matters.

What I then observed of these remarkably sagacious creatures prepared me the more readily to believe the accounts I have since read of their wonderful instincts and habits. That they are carnivorous I inferred from the fact of their invariably drawing into their haunts the dead flies and other insects with which I frequently supplied them. That they moreover have a ready and certain method of communicating intelligence I concluded, from observing that when a solitary ant fell in with the food I had laid in the neighbourhood of the colony, it would first endeavour to draw it home without help, but if it were unable to do this it would go away, and shortly afterwards several others would make their appearance, by whose united and apparently systematic exertions the work was both judiciously and quickly accomplished.

Another of my favourite outdoor amusements was to repose in the shade in the noon-tide of the hot summer days, and watch the flight of the swallows, whose rapid movements and varied evolutions would sometimes astonish me. I was equally pleased with their note, which, though it is both shrill and monotonous, is, I think, not unpleasing, especially when heard in the stillness of a summer's noon. I know not how it may affect others, but with me it has ever had the effect of tranquillizing my feelings. On this account, among others, this bird is among my favourites of the feathered tribes.

Nor must I forget the rooks, of which a colony was settled near to our dwelling. The cawing of these birds, though unpleasant to most people, has always been a source of pleasing emotion to myself. At the time here referred to, I was much accustomed to watch their motions and habits, some of which are not a little curious, and are well worth observing by every one who can sympathise with the enjoyments of the lower animals. I could even now derive much entertainment from observing the movements of these birds, especially while engaged in building or repairing their nests, when all is noise, bustle, and industry through the whole community. Many a time have I been highly diverted with their contests about a twig, which, after being equally claimed by two or more of the architects, has in the heat of the contest been dropped to the ground, and thus made it necessary that each should go in quest of another. I may as well add here that I have frequently found these aërial quarrels to be useful, having thereby been enabled to increase the stock of fallen twigs which I was collecting for household use. Whether by rook-law I had a right to these nest-building materials, I know not; but as they fell upon the king's highway, and, moreover, were never reclaimed by their proprietors, I hope that I committed no great offence in thus appropriating the property of my feathered neighbours.

Ere I pass on, I will just notice one or two more of my juvenile recreations. One of these was to place myself in a reclining posture, and look up into the clear blue sky, which, especially when its uniformity was relieved by a few fleecy clouds, was to me a beautiful spectacle. It suggested the elevating idea of an ascent without a summit, while it seemed to lead to another world—a brighter and happier one than this. At other times I found pleasure in contemplating the reflection of the sky and the clouds, as shown in a vessel of clear water. Here the idea of a descent without a bottom would sometimes present itself to my imagination, and so forcibly as almost to make me recoil from the object that produced it. Yet there was an undefinable charm about this visionary scene, which prompted me to survey it again. I have sometimes done this until it seemed to be a reality, and I have wished it were possible to explore the "vast profound."

My father used to raise a good number of the climbing beans familiarly called "scarlet runners," which he so trained as to make them form a rude arbour. This supplied me with a very convenient retreat in my leisure hours, as here I could be free from interruption. I spent many a pleasant hour in this quiet nook, employed in my favourite amusement. Among the few books at my command was a borrowed copy of Hervey's 'Meditations,' a book well adapted to please the youthful imagination. It pleased mine greatly. Its florid style, although a fault, I much admired, and cannot but think that it was useful in helping to qualify me for perusing in an intelligent manner the far more correct and elegant writings of other authors. Among these I may name Young and Thomson, whose principal poems not long afterwards came into my hands.

Here I must dismiss the subject of amusements, and turn to matters of business. When the time of my going to school was ended, the question arose how I should be disposed of so as to be made useful. I was much too feeble to be put to any very laborious occupation, while my parents were too poor to be able to apprentice me to any suitable trade. Thus there seemed to be no good prospect in regard to my future lot. I was indeed still young, being not more than twelve and a half years old; yet I felt that it was high time to be learning something by which to get a living. After much thought it occurred to me that I might perhaps obtain one in the capacity of a domestic servant.

To this occupation therefore my wishes were directed, but no situation could for a time be procured. Meanwhile my mother kept me employed in the usual way; besides which I undertook the task of teaching my sister the elements of writing and arithmetic. I also endeavoured to carry on the work of self-instruction, both in these and other respects. Yet, as I saw that neither of these exercises would procure me a maintenance, I was but "ill at ease" in regard to either present circumstances or future prospects.

At length, with the consent of my parents, I went out to seek employment. I did this, however, with much diffidence, being conscious of my inability to do any work that required either much strength or skill. After some fruitless inquiries, I at length succeeded in getting employment. This was to look after some horses that were feeding off the hedge-rows in a potato-field. They were tethered to the hedge, and my duty was to tether them in a fresh place when they had eaten all the forage within their reach. I managed to do this pretty well, although at first with much timidity, as I was but little acquainted with the art of managing horses. Ere long, however, I acquired some courage, and, in the end, more than was consistent with discretion, for on untethering one of the horses in order to give him fresh pasturage, it came into my head that I should like to ride him for a short time. The wish was soon followed by a determination to gratify it, and accordingly I mounted him. He was a powerful beast, and, as I soon discovered, of a vicious temper. As I had never been on a horse's back, I was ill prepared to control an animal like this, if he became restive, especially as I had only a halter to hold him by. The result was, that he quickly threw me off, and ran away, leaving me much frightened, but not so severely hurt as I might have expected to be. The horse remained at liberty until my master came into the field. I was mildly reproved for my fault, and retained in my employment until all the hedge-rows were fed off, when I was discharged. From this adventure I learned a little prudence, which was of great use to me when subsequently it became a part of my duty to attempt managing a horse.

Seeing my ill success, my parents resolved to wait patiently until some suitable occupation could be procured for me; I therefore continued to perform my usual duties, with no other variety than that of an occasional journey with my worthy master, when he went from home on his land-measuring business.

At length, however, a place was found for me, to which I went on July 1, 1805, at which time I was not quite thirteen years old. Here I continued until I was qualified to be my own master. My going to this situation I regard as having been by far the most important incident of my early years, inasmuch as all my subsequent experience took its general complexion therefrom. Perhaps, therefore, I may be forgiven if I somewhat minutely describe its duties.

My master was a woollen-draper, in a good way of business. He also carried on the trade of a tailor, but as he did not understand this, he employed a man to manage it for him. My wages were three shillings and sixpence per week, and I had a few trifling perquisites, which might amount to about fourpence more. My parents provided me with food, clothing, and lodging, so that my remuneration was small, considering the amount of labour I had to give in exchange. My duties were neither few nor pleasant; for I was expected to be ready at the call of not fewer than twenty-one persons, namely, my master and mistress, five children, two maid-servants, a shopman, two apprentices, a foreman, and eight journeymen. I hardly need say that I always found it difficult and sometimes impossible to please this large number of people. I honestly endeavoured to please all, but in my well-meant efforts to do this I often, like the old man in the fable, failed to satisfy any one, and consequently was in rather general disgrace, to my great discomfort and discouragement.

I eventually saw that I had been toiling at a hopeless task, and therefore resolved thenceforth to do the best I could, without troubling myself about the consequences.

I soon perceived the propriety of this resolution, as thereby I gained an increase of personal comfort, while I gave quite as much satisfaction as before, to all such as were not unreasonable in their demands. My first care was to please my master and mistress, who were very exact in all their affairs; but as I always had a strong predilection for order and regularity in everything with which I was concerned, I found no great difficulty in pleasing them.

The children were not backward in claiming my services, yet I had no reason to complain of the manner in which they treated me. One of them, indeed, treated me with remarkable kindness, both then and subsequently, as I shall have occasion to notice in the sequel.

The maid-servants were worthy persons, for whom I readily did all the little services I could, and thus secured not only their good will, but also their active kindness, for they frequently gave me what was very acceptable to a hungry boy. I had but little encouragement to serve the shopman and apprentices further than I was obliged, for they often made me do nearly all their share of the shopwork, while they were either quite idle or employed about some trifling matter.

The tailors were rough masters, but in general they were not unreasonable. Most of them, including the foreman, were very ignorant men; while all were, more or less, of dissolute habits. As my chief occupation was in matters connected with the tailoring business, I was necessarily much in the workshop, where usually I saw and heard not a little of what was either foolish or wicked.

It was truly, as all such places are, a perilous school for an inexperienced boy, and the consequences might have been injurious to my future welfare had I been predisposed to what I here either witnessed or heard commended. I believe that I escaped with but little moral injury; yet I was often much perplexed by the effect produced upon me by the obscene and profane language which I so frequently heard. As to the latter, I was a good deal disturbed about it, for several months after I was first accustomed to hear it. The oaths I heard in the shop seemed to be almost incessantly sounding in my ears, until I began to suspect that I was making them my own. This troubled me much, for I really feared an oath. After some time, however, I was less painfully affected in this way; but I then encountered another difficulty. I perceived that I could hear the most awful curses and imprecations without being much shocked, and I attributed this want of feeling if not to a concealed approbation of swearing, yet to an inadequate sense of its enormity.

I subsequently discovered that my seeming indifference arose from a cause over which I had little if any control, namely, the force of habit, under the influence of which I have since then often heard unmoved the most fearful oaths that perhaps it is possible for either man or demon to utter. Yet I have always deprecated the use of profane language. I have indeed ever regarded it as being equally senseless and wicked; and, moreover, can safely affirm that I have never allowed myself to use one, nor for many years past any asseveration stronger than Yea or Nay, unless when required to swear judicially.

I will just add here, that there are many worthy people who unconsciously use highly exceptionable phrases. They would no longer allow themselves to say "'zounds," "'ods-pottikins," "'sdeath," and such like words, did they but know that under this unmeaning and, as they imagine, harmless jargon, there are concealed some of the profanest and most revolting expressions that can possibly be uttered.

Obscene discourse I equally dislike; it has indeed been the object of "my most implacable disgust" even from my early years. I have heard so much of both this and of profane swearing, that I now "hate them with a perfect hatred."

I have said that my duties were numerous as well as onerous. This will be manifest when I state the various items which entered into the account of each day's labour. My regular working-hours were from five o'clock in the morning until after sunset during summer, and from daybreak until about nine o'clock in the evening during the winter, abating half an hour at breakfast-time and an hour for dinner. But when work was plentiful or was wanted by any given time, I was required to be at the shop both earlier and later than the hours here named. My first business in the morning was to sweep the workshop, kindle the fire used for heating the pressing-irons, sift coals and cinder-ashes in order to get coal-dust and cinders for fuel, clean several dozens of knives and forks, and sometimes assist in opening and cleaning the woollen-drapery shop. When I had got through these jobs it was time to get my breakfast. After I had done this, I was generally employed by the tailors in fetching the irons, tending the fire in which they were heated, matching cloth or trimmings, brushing clothes, or cleaning buttons. I was also frequently sent out with parcels of cloth or with clothes; in fact, I was kept almost incessantly occupied until dinner-time. My afternoon's duties were not much different from those of the morning, either in number or kind, except that I was then sent, perhaps several times, to the public-house to get beer for the tailors. Sometimes I was sorely annoyed by this extra duty, not only because I disliked their half-drunken frolics, but also because I was hereby deprived of nearly all the little leisure which fell to my lot; the time for this, when it did offer, being commonly in the latter part of the afternoon, which was just the time that the men chose for their drinking bouts. After they had left work it was my further duty to shut up the shop, put out the fire, and take home such garments as were wanted by the customers. Before I could get through these matters it was high time to get my supper, and prepare for bed.

It will hence appear that I had but little time to spare for my own use. This, however, was a privation which, of all others, I was the least willing to endure. I wanted a little reading time, and as I had none allowed me, I determined upon making some. For this purpose I arose earlier from bed, read while walking or eating, and took care not to waste the spare minutes which sometimes fell to my lot in the course of my working-hours. By these means I saved more time in the aggregate than I had previously thought to be possible. It was indeed made up of fragments, yet I contrived to make it answer my purposes. I had been made the more anxious to get some spare time, because several books which I had not before seen now fell in my way. This was through the courtesy of my young master, whose kindly feeling I have already noticed. He now gave me free access to his little library, in which were Enfield's 'Speaker,' Goldsmith's 'Geography,' an abridged 'History of Rome,' a 'History of England,' Thomson's 'Seasons,' 'The Citizen of the World,' 'The Vicar of Wakefield,' and some other books the titles of which I do not now remember.

These books furnished me with a large amount of amusing and instructive reading. I perused each of them with much interest, but especially the 'Seasons.' I found this to be just the book I had long wanted. It commended itself to my warmest approbation, immediately on my perceiving its character and design. I do not go beyond the truth when I state that the perusal of this volume was of great use to me in the way of preserving me from the depraved tastes and habits of those with whom my duty compelled me to associate. When I was about fifteen years old, I bought a miniature copy, which from that time until I had reached the age of twenty years I usually kept in my pocket. It was my custom to read each poem in that season of the year to which it refers, as thereby I could the more fully enter into its spirit, and the more easily remember what I read.

With the exception of the Bible, I know not that I ever read any other book so attentively and regularly. Its beautiful descriptions of nature were delightful to my imagination, while its fine moral reflections—its earnest dissuasives from vice—and its persuasive exhortations to virtue, were, as I believe, greatly instrumental in promoting my best interests.

The pleasure with which I at first perused the 'Seasons' was much enhanced by an illusion quite natural to an imaginative and inexperienced mind. I did not then know that the poet's business is rather to present pictures of what ought to be than of what really is; and therefore I regarded Thomson's beautiful and impressive descriptions of rural life and manners as being strictly in accordance with existing realities. I was indeed conscious that there was in my own case something wanted, and which must be supplied before it would be possible for me to realize the happiness of which the poet speaks. What this was I did not immediately perceive, but after a little cogitation it occurred to me that "an elegant sufficiency" of worldly riches would enable me to procure much of what would tend to make me happy. I was then simple enough to imagine that this was attainable even by such a one as myself: this, however, was a delusion under which it was scarcely possible I should long continue. In a comparatively short time I discovered my mistake, and thenceforward read Thomson and other poets with less of romantic feeling, but, I think, with more of genuine pleasure. I can hardly tell how it was that the vanishing of all my pleasing visions affected me so slightly as it did, but perhaps it might be owing to my thoughts being about this time directed in an especial manner to the contemplation of another state of existence.* By some secret process I was led to acquiesce in my appointed lot; to give up the hope of obtaining perfect happiness in this life, and to aspire after the nobler pleasures of another and a fairer state of being. From this time I began to contemplate nature under a new aspect, and with different feelings than before. I was increasingly charmed with every magnificent

* I was then about fifteen years old.

or beautiful scene or object, because it served to remind me of the far grander or lovelier realities of the invisible world; but for the habit of regarding the beauties of the visible creation as the "shadows or symbols of heavenly things," they would long ere now have ceased to afford me any real pleasure, so entirely has a long course of personal suffering destroyed my power of enjoying even the fairest scenes, unless it be possible to connect them in my imagination with that world where there is " no more pain." Looking, however, as I do, upon " the things that are seen " as the representatives or types of " the things that are not seen," I am sometimes, in spite of all my infirmities, enabled to contemplate a sublime or beautiful object or prospect with emotions of heartfelt and elevating pleasure.

Having repeatedly adverted to the beauty which is perceptible by the eye, I will take occasion to notice that which is perceived by the ear. Considering what I have stated concerning my love of poetry, the intelligent reader will not be surprised when I tell him that I have always been passionately fond of music, both vocal and instrumental: of the latter none has ever pleased me more than that of church bells. With this I have always been greatly moved, but the emotion varies much in its character, according to the particular time at which I hear the music, or the circumstances in which I am *then* placed. Thus in the morning, especially if the weather be fine, the ringing of bells inspires me with a cheerfulness of which at other times I am unconscious: visions of joyful and happy scenes forthwith present themselves to the fancy and refresh the heart. At mid-day the same music fails to affect me in so lively a manner; I cannot then get so far clear of the world's cares or toils or uproar, as to be able to interpret aright the meaning of its delightful yet mystical tones. In the evening it awakens emotions of either a solemn or a pensive kind, yet they are such as I would not willingly exchange for all the light-heartedness of the gay and the thoughtless. Perhaps I never had these feelings more fully excited than on a fine summer evening many years ago, when the church bells were rung in compliment to a large body of troops which at that unusual hour was marching out of the town in order to go upon foreign service. On this occasion the music, although in itself of a lively character, seemed to me like a solemn anticipatory dirge in honour of the brave men who were about to encounter the horrors and the dangers of war, and of whom many would doubtless fall in the coming conflict. I was the more tenderly touched because of the mistimed gaiety of many among the doomed victims, and also because of the senseless merriment of the accompanying crowds. My thoughts, meanwhile, were forcibly turned to the already bereaved parents, together with the wives and children whose hearts, not without reason, were then sinking in sadness deep and inexpressible, while all around them were revelling in the full tide of seeming enjoyment and exultation. I have always found pleasure in hearing the bells chime in token of the approaching celebration of public worship, but have been especially pleased with the clear and solemn tones of the single bell which, to use a familiar provincial phrase, "tolls in" the congregation. There is one particular bell to the tones of which I have both so often and so intently listened, that I think I should be able to recognise them wherever they might strike upon my ear. This bell belongs to one of the churches in my native town; it has always seemed to me to be singularly musical, and to be expressive of hallowed thoughts and feelings. Whether it announced the coming hour of public devotion, or the departure from this world of a kindred spirit, or the approaching interment of some faded human form, I was equally, although differently moved. Either the beatific worship of the heavenly state, or the condition of separate spirits in general, or the mysteries of death, were hereby suggested to my mind; and thus I was led into trains of thought and feeling such as I would fain recall in all their original power and solemnity. The music of bells at midnight affects my imagination in a peculiarly forcible manner. It invariably carries me in thought far beyond this "visible diurnal sphere," to that bright and happy world from whence I could almost believe it to emanate: I seem as if I could fancy it to be the distant echo of that sublime chorus which is said to have resembled "the sound of many waters," or that which our heaven-taught bard tells us was

> "Loud as from numbers without number; sweet
> As from blest voices uttering joy."

I must now mention some other books which about this time fell in my way. Among these an odd volume of the 'Spectator' deserves particular notice. Where it came from, or to whom it belonged, I never knew: I discovered it in my master's kitchen. On opening it I was struck by the seeming oddity of its contents. As the book promised to give me a little amusement, I forthwith set about reading it. I was at first a good deal mystified about its author, character, and design; yet I was much gratified with it. For some time I thought it to be the work of only one person, who chose to conceal himself under a feigned name. I was somewhat disconcerted on afterwards discovering that the work was the joint production of several persons; for I had drawn an amusing imaginary picture of both the author and the places he frequented. I moreover felt a good deal of sympathy with his professed habits and pursuits; but found, as has since then happened to me in far more vexatious matters, that I had been pleasing myself with a shadow. This however, after all, was but a trifling drawback upon the amusement which the volume afforded me.

When I had made myself pretty well acquainted with the contents of this stray volume, I was strongly desirous of reading the entire work. This, however, I could not then do, except by hiring it—which would have caused an expense to which my purse was not equal: but so soon as I could afford this indulgence, I procured the remaining seven volumes, which I found to be equally interesting; and I was not fully satisfied until I had gone through the whole series a third time. From this singularly amusing and instructive work I gleaned various scraps of knowledge, which perhaps have been as useful to me as these several readings were entertaining. It was here that

I caught a few glimpses of the world, which served to prepare me for the better threading its mazes in after-life. I have, since then, met with many living and forcible exemplifications of the truths promulged by the "Spectator" and his "Companions;" and have been struck with the faithfulness of their pictures of human nature, under many of its numerous and ever-changing aspects. Without being conscious of the fact, I was, while only looking for amusement, receiving real instruction upon many important points of both principle and practice—instruction for which I have since had much occasion to be grateful. Here also I found help in the way of rightly understanding the noble work of our great epic poet. The criticisms of Mr. Addison upon the 'Paradise Lost' led me to give it an attentive reading, in the course of which I became much interested in its argument. But the pleasure I derived from this source was a good deal alloyed by the pain I felt at the catastrophe of the poem. I was conscious of a personal interest in this sad issue; which consciousness, for a time, was accompanied by feelings far too painful to be easily described. It was not until I had got rid of these unpleasant emotions that I could fully enjoy the perusal of this wonderful performance. Whether or not a perfect epic poem ought to close with the full and permanent triumph of its hero, is a question which I have neither ability nor occasion to determine; but whatever may be its true solution, I cannot subscribe to Mr. Dryden's opinion that "Satan" is the real hero of the 'Paradise Lost.' It is with diffidence that I venture to differ from so high an authority, yet I cannot help thinking that if his opinion were well grounded, it would go far towards destroying the reader's interest in the poem. I may just notice here the answer which Mr. Addison makes to the objection that the 'Paradise Lost' is not an heroic poem. He says, "Those who will not give it that title, may call it, if they please, a divine poem. It will be sufficient for its perfection if it has in it all the beauties of the highest kind of poetry ; and as for those who allege it is not an heroic poem, they advance no more to the diminution of it, than if they should say Adam is not Æneas, nor Eve Helen."*

* I ought, perhaps, to state that I write these memoirs wholly from memory, and therefore shall probably omit to record some matters connected with my early years, which it might be well to glance at. This, however, is a difficulty which I cannot now obviate, but must simply do the best I can.

CHAPTER IV.

I THINK it was somewhere about the time to which the preceding notices refer, that my thoughts were first directed to political questions. Until then I had not been in the way of hearing anything respecting them. I had, indeed, heard a good deal of vague talk about the peace of 1802 and the preparations for war in 1803—together with many remarks about the probable consequences of that contest. Moreover, I was not quite ignorant of military affairs; yet I had no clear perception of the connection between these things and the interests of either Great Britain or any other country. It was generally affirmed that it was a good thing to beat the French, but as to either the quality or the extent of this asserted good I was totally uninformed. It was at the general election in 1806 that I was induced to inquire a little into the meaning of all the bustle and parade which I witnessed during the contest for representing my native town in parliament. Herein I was assisted by my friendly young master; he could not, indeed, answer all my queries, but he was able to give me as much information as enabled me to form some idea of the matter. My informant was even then, as he has ever since been, a warm friend of the Whig party; while all the other members of the family were hearty partisans of the Tories.

" I know not that I ever saw a newspaper in my father's house during the whole term of my early years: a fragment of one would, indeed, sometimes find its way thither. From this source, however, I could have got but little information, even had I sought it—which I do not remember to have done. Now, however, I began to pry into the contents of "this folio of four pages" whenever it came in my way. My master—in conjunction with some friends —took in a newspaper, called, if I remember rightly, 'Lloyd's Evening Post;' and at this I sometimes got a hasty peep. At first, as was natural, I was chiefly interested with the domestic news: I took care to read about

"The moving accidents by fire or flood,"

with an account of which a newspaper commonly abounds. But my curiosity was not long confined to these "little things." It soon led me to look at the articles of foreign intelligence, which—as it was a time of almost universal war—were full of strange and spirit-stirring narrations. From these the transition was easy to the perusal of the parliamentary news, together with the speeches delivered at public meetings, and, ere long, I could take pleasure in reading about

"The grand debate,
The popular harangue, the tart reply,
The logic, and the wisdom, and the wit,
And the loud laugh,"

which, from time to time, I here found to be recorded. At length I ventured upon reading what are called the leading articles, together with whatever else touched upon public affairs. From that period until now—although without ever having been a mere newsmonger—I have always felt a lively interest in looking over the contents of a newspaper. I will just add, that he must be a careless reader who does not turn even this light reading to some good account.

Somewhere about this time I met with a volume to which I am much indebted. This was a copy of Simpson's 'Plea for Religion and the Sacred Writings'—concerning which I have heard it said that it ought rather to have been called 'A Plea for Infidelity,' because of its dwelling so much upon the corruptions of Christianity and the inconsistent deportment of some among its ministers. This objection, however, did not strike me as being of any real force, for I perceived—what, indeed, is self-evident—that the errors or even the vices of men can in nowise disprove the reality of religion nor invalidate its claims. The immoral practices of professed Christians may be satisfactorily and readily accounted for, without calling in question either the facts or the doctrines of Christianity. Yet I have long thought that it would have been as well if the estimable author of this book had been less minute in his accounts of the misdeeds of men professing the Christian faith; for notwithstanding the plain fact that Christianity and its corruptions are totally distinct and separate matters, it is certain that many persons seem to be quite unable to perceive the difference between them. But it is not my business to be a critic: I have to do with the book only so far as it had any influence upon myself. In my case it was a seasonable defence against the perils to which both my principles and morals were exposed from my constant association with persons who were greatly hostile to moral truth and thoroughly careless about moral virtue. Besides all this, I owe to this volume many scraps of knowledge upon various subjects referred to in the notes by which the text is appropriately and extensively illustrated.

Nor must I omit to mention the obligations I owe to some essays written by the late Rev. Thomas Scott, and which were given me by my master. I do not remember their exact titles, nor can I recollect much of more than one of them. This was, if I err not, a kind of exposition of the tenth commandment. From the author's forcible statements respecting the nature of covetousness, and the various ways in which this passion develops itself, I became partly convinced that all games of chance or hazard, for the sake of pecuniary gain, were morally wrong. This partial conviction settled into a fixed and hitherto unalterable belief—a belief, moreover, which has governed my practice. I have seen much of gambling, and have heard much said in its praise, especially in regard to both state lotteries and what were called "little goes," together with Tontines and the like; yet I have never staked even the smallest sum upon the issue of any game or speculation whatever. Neither have I sought for amusement from any species of gaming, for I have seen much of the occasions hereby given for bringing into play some of the worst passions of human nature. I have never witnessed the display of more hateful feelings nor ever heard more profane language uttered than on the occasion of a game where the stake was *nothing*.

I now turn, for a while, from books to men and manners—of both which I had at this time considerable opportunities of taking notice. Having already given a brief sketch of my master, together with his numerous household and workmen, I shall forbear saying further about them than merely to remark that the general conversation and deportment of the latter were such as denoted them to be lovers of themselves rather than of God or of their fellow-men. I was sometimes sent to the houses of such of them as were married men, where, in general, I failed to witness the marks of good housewifery which, amidst all my mother's troubles and privations, were ever apparent in herself, her children, and her humble dwelling. I could not but perceive the difference, and I learned thereby the more fully to approve of cleanliness, decency, and good order, and, moreover, to regard their opposites as being the proper objects of deep and lasting disapprobation. I was also frequently sent to the barracks with clothes for the officers who employed my master. In the rooms of some of these gentlemen I sometimes witnessed what put me to the blush; and I have since then wondered that full-grown men—and gentlemen too—should have permitted such conduct to come within the notice of one like myself.

I need not dwell upon the yet more degrading actions and the disgusting language of the private soldiers and their companions. Among these I could not but perceive that

> "Vice is a creature of such hateful mien,
> As, to be hated, needs but to be seen."

I forbear to mention the numbers or the names of the regiments to which these depraved men belonged. There was much difference between one regiment and another in regard to both moral character and becoming deportment. But I must not omit to name some that were distinguished by the truly gentleman-like bearing of the officers, and the almost universal sobriety and civility of the privates. These were the 42nd, the 79th, and the 92nd regiments of the line,* each of which was composed of Scottish Highlanders—or, at least, of Scotchmen. They were bodies of really soldier-like, well-behaved, and otherwise respectable men, who both acquired and retained the respect of their fellow-soldiers and also of the inhabitants of the town and its neighbourhood.

The general election consequent upon the breaking up of Lord Grenville's administration, in the spring of 1807, gave me the means of adding a little more to my knowledge of the world. I could not, indeed, interpret rightly all that I saw and heard, but I could, nevertheless, understand enough thereof to see the instability of popular favour, and the

* To which might be added the 95th (a rifle corps), whose commander, at the time here referred to, was a fine example of the Christian gentleman, as well as of the efficient military officer.

worthlessness of popular applause. The gentleman who had been the favourite candidate of the people, and whom they had joyfully sent into Parliament less than a year before, was now so coldly received by his recent friends, that he thought it prudent to retire from the field without trying the issue of a contest. The watchwords which he so effectively employed at the preceding election—" T———l and the glorious Revolution of 1688"—were now powerless, while those of his opponent—" No Popery "—appeared to have an almost talismanic influence. The worthy (?) electors seemed to have undergone a transformation which, to the uninitiated in such matters, was not easily to be accounted for. Except from the speeches and placards of the candidates and their friends, I should not then have discovered that the exercise of the elective franchise involves the discharge of a public duty; neither should I have judged it to be conducive to any real private advantage. From the general aspect of the whole scene I should rather have inferred that it was considered merely as an occasion for indulging in unrestrained intemperance and lawless confusion.

The countenance which I saw was given to these and other immoral practices by respectable men was what I could not understand; and even now I am at a loss to comprehend fully how it is that such men can allow themselves to patronize what has so powerful a tendency to debase the character and to injure the condition of their unreflecting and needy countrymen.

The next public event that attracted my notice was

the great military expedition to Copenhagen. Nearly if not all the regiments of the line then in the adjacent barracks were sent upon this service; and I think it was the bustle and excitement connected with their departure that led my master's workmen to take some additional interest in public affairs. Until this time I do not remember to have heard them talk much about matters of that description. Now, however, they clubbed their pence to pay for a newspaper, and selected the 'Weekly Political Register' of that clever man the late William Cobbett. This journal was in the form of a pamphlet. It was chiefly filled with the letters of correspondents and the political disquisitions of the proprietor. The only news it contained was that which related to the naval and military operations of the British forces. The 'Political Register' was soon thought to be deficient in matters of general interest. It was therefore exchanged for the 'Courier,' which in a short time gave place to the 'Independent Whig.' From this time the men were warm politicians—not indeed very well conversant with public affairs, but what they lacked in knowledge they made up by a rather large amount of zealous partisanship. When they were too busy to look over the newspaper they employed me as their reader—an office whose duties I found to be very pleasant.

About this time I might also have had a little amusement of a more active description, but for my timidity and unskilfulness. My master kept a horse, which occasionally required to be taken out for the purpose of giving him exercise. It usually fell to my lot to be sent out with him—a task from which I might perhaps have been excused had I told master that I was not equal to its due performance. I was, however, ashamed to do this, and consequently was several times brought into much danger; for although the horse was not a much better-looking animal than was Don Quixote's Rosinante, or the renowned Grizzle of Dr. Syntax, he was nevertheless a good deal self-willed, and moreover had sufficient acuteness to perceive that I was neither skilful nor strong enough to manage him. He therefore did nearly as he pleased with his rider. Several times he ran away with me. On these occasions he ran just as long and in just such a direction as it pleased him. Meanwhile I had quite enough to do to keep my seat. In order to secure this I adopted a plan resembling that of my famous predecessor, John Gilpin, with only this difference, that whereas John held fast by his horse's mane, I kept firm hold of the saddle; yet with even this precaution I was once nearly unseated by being brought into contact with a brewer's dray, while on another occasion I was fairly brought to the ground. In this latter instance I was in considerable danger. My horse became frightened at the cackling of some geese, on which (without giving me any further notice than that of squeaking in a tone much resembling that of a pig, which was his usual note of preparation for a frolic) he set off at full gallop. I was soon dismounted; but being fearful that I should not easily catch him if he got clear away, I retained my hold of the bridle, and thus was trailed a considerable distance. I can hardly tell how I recovered my standing, or contrived to get the better of my wayward steed; but happily I did both, without sustaining much damage further than that of being dirty. The effect of this accident was that I became a yet more timid rider than ever. I endeavoured indeed to become a better horseman, but with hardly any success. The chief difficulty I encountered was in keeping my seat when the horse changed his pace from either a walk or a canter to a trot. In each of these cases I was in danger of being thrown off by the suddenness of the shock thereby produced. I escaped this result only by keeping a firm hold of the saddle, but I was sometimes prevented doing this by not being on my guard. In addition to these inconveniences I had frequently to bear the ridicule of both men and boys, who, perceiving my awkwardness, did not fail to rally me thereupon in a way which I felt to be not a little embarrassing. It were needless to dwell upon the satisfaction with which I at length received my discharge from these equestrian exercises. Only once since then have I mounted a horse, and this was sorely against my will, but I could not well avoid it, although I feared it might lead me to re-enact some of my former feats.

My pedestrian expeditions were in general less hazardous, yet one of these was attended by circumstances which I felt to be a good deal embarrassing. It was necessary that some clothes should be sent home which were not finished until late in the day, and as I had a considerable distance to go, I was benighted long before I got to my journey's end. It was a dark winter's evening. Part of my path led through a narrow dirty lane, across the bottom of which ran a river, then much swollen by the late heavy rains. A bridge, formed of only two planks in width, with a hand-rail on one side, was the only means of getting to the farther side of the stream. It was not an easy matter to find this bridge in a night so dark as this was. I had taken the precaution of carrying with me a lantern, but just as I came close upon the river my light was extinguished. This mishap threw me into no small perplexity. I was afraid to go forward, I dared not return without performing my errand, and I had no means of procuring a light. In this dilemma I bethought myself of a farm-house not far from where I was, and immediately set about trying to find it. This was a rather difficult task, but at length I accomplished it, and procured a light.

This, to some, may appear to be an incident so trifling as to be hardly worth recording. To such I would say, that it involved my personal safety, and might as easily have had a fatal termination as if the circumstances attending it had been of a more extraordinary character.

On another occasion I was sent to a village about four miles distant, my path to which was upon the top of a clay-wall, which kept the stream it bounded from overflowing the neighbouring marshes. It was winter-time,—there was much snow on the ground,—the ditches, pools, and (in some places) the river also, were covered with ice. There was a cutting wind, and I was but thinly clad. I remember to have felt cold and cheerless, as I wended my way through a scene which to me seemed dreary and desolate. When I approached the place of my destination I found that I had taken the wrong path; for the river, which I ought to have crossed at the outset of my walk, now rolled betwixt me and the place in question. The only way of getting over was by a ferry-boat; but here a new difficulty presented itself, for I had no money. The ferry-man was not to be moved by a tale of distress, but insisted upon having his fare, in either hard cash or goods. I had nothing wherewith to satisfy his demands, except a pocket-knife; this, therefore, I left with him as a pledge until my return. I then redeemed it, with a penny borrowed of the good man to whom I had been sent.

This journey was the means of giving my health a shock from which it has never yet recovered, nor ever will recover. My feeble and much overworked frame was ill-prepared for an encounter with the "biting frost" and the bitterly cold wind which then assailed it; and the consequence was, that I soon afterwards became seriously ill. I was confined to my dwelling, and in a great degree to my bed, for five weeks, during the greater part of which time it was very doubtful whether I should ever again go abroad. The chief symptoms were, a severe cough, copious night-sweats, much debility, and loss of appetite. I do not remember that I had any medical advice or assistance, until towards the close of the five weeks above referred to. My parents did their best to promote both my comfort and my restoration to health; but all they were able to do amounted to but little, on account of their straitened circumstances. These were now made still narrower by the loss of my wages, which, though small, were yet an important addition to their scanty income. All they received during my illness, in abatement of their loss, was two shillings and a small piece of mutton. I say not this in the way of complaint, much less of reproach; for my master was not a rich man, while he had to bear the heavy charges of a numerous family, none of whom were able to contribute anything towards the maintenance of the household. I should not, indeed, have noted down these particulars, but for the light they throw upon circumstances which, although very common, are nevertheless much overlooked. I refer to the peculiar difficulties attendant upon the illness of working people, who, when their condition requires increased comforts, are, by the failure of their income, frequently rendered unable to procure even the common necessaries of life. For myself I can safely affirm that I felt not a little of this privation during the illness of which I have been writing, and I have good reason to believe that I feel the consequences thereof even at the present time. Yet, disastrous as it was to my easily shaken frame, there was an admixture of good with the evil. This good was of a moral kind; and was, as I believe, both genuine and enduring. My illness had the effect of moderating my wishes and hopes respecting temporal happiness, which, until then, like those of most young people, were far too sanguine. Whether or not my disorder was such as to warrant the fear of a fatal termination, I cannot say; thus much, however, is certain, that I for some time apprehended this issue, and endeavoured to prepare for it.

In this I was much more successful at the time

than I could have expected; and from then, until now, I have never been much moved at the thought of dissolution: neither have I thought the contemplation of death to be a melancholy task. Should any one be curious to know how this effect was produced, I hesitate not to affirm that it was through the medium of a cordial belief in that volume which brings " life and immortality to light." In the cheering announcements of this book I was enabled to see

> " Death of its sting disarm'd, and the dark grave
> Made pervious to the realms of endless day."

How little do they who neglect or refuse to avail themselves of the consolations of Christianity, know of the costly sacrifice which they thus make to their own thoughtlessness or prejudice! What else is there that can either irradiate the mind or animate the heart, when shrouded in the gloomy atmosphere of those "days of darkness" which, sooner or later, come upon every human being? In how many seasons of acute suffering or of depressing languor have I been soothed or supported by such declarations as these:—" The inhabitant of that land shall no more say, 'I am sick:'"—" And there shall be no more death; neither sorrow, nor crying: neither shall there be any more pain." But I forbear to enlarge upon this subject. To the wise a word will be enough; while to the unwise even a multitude of words, although they were "most eloquent," would be but as an empty sound.

CHAPTER V.

The serious thoughts to which my illness gave rise were much strengthened by my reading at the time several of Dr. Watts's 'Lyric Poems,'* which then first came into my hands. The reader will, perhaps, bear with me if I quote a passage which then was, and at many subsequent times has been, the means of awakening much encouraging thought:—

> " The past temptations
> No more shall vex us; ev'ry grief we feel
> Shortens the destin'd number; ev'ry pulse
> Beats a sharp moment of the pain away,
> And the last stroke will come. By swift degrees
> Time sweeps us off, and we shall soon arrive
> At life's sweet period—O celestial point
> That ends this mortal story."

I resumed my work at the earliest possible time; but was in a very unfit state for the fatigue I was obliged to undergo. I was much enfeebled, and,

---

* The volume containing these belonged to the edition of the British Poets which was published by that enterprising bookseller Mr. Cooke. It was, I think, the first edition of these authors' works which united a moderate price with good paper, clear printing, and tasteful embellishments. There were (in fact) two editions, both of which were published in numbers; the best, with proof impressions of the plates, and printed upon a fine paper, was sold at a shilling, and the inferior one at sixpence, per number. It is much to be regretted that Mr. Cooke should have met the fate—far too frequent—of liberal-minded publishers.

moreover, breathed with considerable difficulty; besides which, I was troubled with a distressing cough. I now sought medical advice of a kind-hearted physician. This gentleman, whose name was Parry, was attached to the forces in the adjacent barracks. He treated me with such kindness, both of language and manner, as to inspire me with feelings of gratitude, which even now have not wholly subsided. He gave me advice as to the taking proper care of myself, and, moreover, some medicine; but I think he perceived that I chiefly needed such physic as that good man Dr. Goldsmith gave to the poor woman who craved his professional aid. From his asking me, very pointedly, whether or not any of my relatives had died of consumption, I inferred that he considered my complaint to be of that character. It turned out, however, to be an asthmatic affection, from which I soon afterwards suffered no small inconvenience, and which through many subsequent years, even down to the present time, has been the bane and burden of my life.

My original suffering from this source would have been much alleviated had I been considerately dealt with by my taskmasters. This, however, was far enough from being the case: I was made to do my full amount of work, just the same as if I had ailed nothing. Notwithstanding my severe cough, and the severity of the weather—for it was winter-time—I was made thoroughly to clean the outside of two large bay-windows that lighted the front-shop; a job that kept me in the open air for two or three hours.

In addition to this, I was compelled by an unfeeling shopman to take the heaviest work in daily opening and closing the shop; also in putting up and taking down weekly a partition which was used on Sundays. His conduct was the more inexcusable, inasmuch as he was a strong and active young man, and moreover was well aware of my weak and disordered state. I forbore to complain of him to my master; but I ventured to remonstrate with my oppressor, who took offence thereat, and thenceforth treated me with increased harshness. Many a time has he made me work hard while I was struggling with a fit of coughing so violent as to produce retching, at which he could be amused. I never complained much of this treatment to my parents, for I well knew that they could not afford to keep me at home, and I was afraid, if I told them all, that their concern for my health and comfort might get the better of their prudence, and thus lead to their making such a remonstrance as would incur the loss of my employment.

If I rightly interpret my present temper, I narrate these circumstances without anything of resentment; but I am free to confess that at the time I was frequently in danger of being angry as well as grieved at the harsh treatment I received. And I further confess that when I, some years afterwards, saw my persecutor's name in a list of bankrupts, I could hardly help considering his disasters as a righteous retribution for the cruelty of which he was formerly guilty towards myself. What became of him after his bankruptcy I do not know; I would, however, hope that he found more sympathy and help in the day of his need than he ever vouchsafed to bestow upon me. I continued in very bad health until the spring-time, when I nearly got rid of my cough, and moreover gained a little strength; but my breathing was frequently very difficult, especially if I attempted to run, or even to walk quickly. I had formerly been rather nimble-footed, but I now found that my running-days were gone by. I have never since then been able to exceed a moderate walking-pace, except for a very short distance. I retained, however, my custom of getting an early morning walk, being prompted thereto by an increasing love for natural beauty, and also by a desire to secure a convenient opportunity for reading and reflection. In these early rambles I often felt that peculiar kind of bodily languor which, so far from being unfavourable to mental activity, seems rather to be instrumental in arousing the mind to

" Solemn thought
And heavenly musing."

At any rate it had this effect upon myself, for whenever it came upon me my thoughts adverted to that state of existence in which the weary and broken-down pilgrims of earth "rest from their labours," and that too for ever. My heart would then yearn after that rest, and I would willingly have encountered all the intermediate conflict with mortal pain and death, in order to obtain it. In these seasons I would gladly have seen Time annihilated as it regarded myself, so that I might at once have been freed from the pains and perils of mortal life. With these feelings—which I do not like to call morbid—it was natural that I should cease to regard death and the grave with anything like terror, or even with aversion. I was, indeed, willing to be familiar with both, and found a strange pleasure in contemplating whatever most forcibly reminded me of them. I have spent many an hour, of a not unpleasing character, in church-yard rambles, and could there witness whatever I saw of human mortality, without wishing to escape the "common lot" of my species.

It was in this state of feeling that I first got hold of a little volume called 'The Wreath,' containing a collection of poems by various authors. Among these pieces was 'The Grave,' which soon commended itself to my hearty and unqualified approbation. For a good while it was to me a sort of bosom-friend, the companion of my leisure hours, the prompter of my meditations while I was at work. It thus became written so deeply upon my memory as not to be easily obliterated. Even now I could, with but little assistance, recite nearly the whole poem. I presume not to scan it critically, yet I may, perhaps, be allowed to say that in many places it appears to me to be true and eloquent poetry.

Besides this poem, the volume contained 'The Minstrel,' of which I venture to say that I consider it to be of almost unequalled beauty and interest. To have been the author of this poem was, as I think, an honour of no common order. To me it has ever appeared to be an exquisitely finished production, adapted equally to the purposes of informing the understanding, ameliorating the passions, and pleasing the imagination. Everything about it pleases me. The structure of the verse—the sentiments—the descriptions—are alike beautiful, and in admirable keeping.

There was here yet another poem which arrested my attention fully as much as did 'The Minstrel' or 'The Grave.' This was entitled 'Death,'—a prize-poem written by that eminently good man Dr. Porteus. It was also in this little volume that I first became acquainted with the poetry of that good but hapless man Christopher Smart. It was one of his prize-poems: I have, since then, read the whole of these fine compositions. Some quotations from Dr. Young's 'Night Thoughts,' which I met with in the 'Plea for Religion' and elsewhere, led me to seek an opportunity for perusing the whole of these compositions. This, however, so far as I can remember, did not offer itself until I contrived to buy a copy. It was a cheap, small volume, and thus was suited both to my purse and to my purpose of carrying it about me. I read it with eagerness, and with emotions such as I am hardly able to characterize aright; but I think they were chiefly those of wonder mingled with delight. Here, moreover, I found ample means of learning how to observe the most magnificent objects of nature, and how to meditate profitably upon many subjects of great interest and importance. Many of the author's thoughts were to me entirely new, and I greatly admired both the noble and the beautiful imagery by which many of them are illustrated. Some of them, indeed, which had not the charm of novelty, were nevertheless made to appear singularly beautiful by reason of the attractive form in which they were for the first time brought before me. I sometimes found it difficult to make out the author's meaning, on account of the peculiarity or the obscurity of his style. This, however, neither displeased nor discouraged me. It served rather to quicken and strengthen my efforts towards fully understanding what was meant. I had in very early life contracted a habit of resolutely endeavouring to understand whatever I might be engaged in; and, as I had generally succeeded in a good degree, I doubted not that I should also succeed in regard to the difficulties which I here encountered. Nor was I disappointed herein, for, ere long, I found that I could perceive pretty clearly the purport of even the most difficult passages, with the exception, however, of *two,* to which, even now, I cannot affix any determinate sense.*

I had never before been led to contemplate the universe under an aspect so magnificent and impressive as that under which I here saw it represented. The earth, together with the whole system of worlds to which it belongs, seemed to be only an atom—almost a nonentity—in comparison with the vast, the

---

* The first is in that section called " The Christian Triumph," and reads thus—

" The great first—last! pavilion'd high he sits
In darkness from excessive splendour, borne
By gods unseen, unless through lustre lost.'

The other is in the third section, and is as follows:—

" And shall we then for virtue's sake commence
Apostates? and turn infidels for joy?"

seemingly unbounded extent of the universal creation. As to myself, I felt that I was almost " less than nothing and vanity;" or, at the most, a unit of very little amount in the vast aggregated sum of created objects.

These impressions fixed themselves upon the mind and became the instruments of much moral benefit. They served to prevent my indulging in self-important or self-gratulatory feelings; while they inspired me with becoming thoughts concerning the majesty and the power, the wisdom and the goodness, of the infinitely great Creator.

The strong tendency of my mind at this time to serious thought was a good deal increased by several incidents in which I felt considerable interest. One of these was the death of the venerable man who was my school-patron, and who for many years had been the officiating minister of the congregation to which I belonged. There was something of unusual ceremony connected with the burial of his remains. One who had been his fellow-student preached his funeral discourse; there was a large assembly of hearers, among which there were many who belonged to other communities, but were now present in token of their respect for the memory of a good man. For several years prior to his decease he had, by the infirmities of age, been laid aside from his pastoral duties. He had procured a colleague, an excellent man, who was reported to be a good scholar and an efficient teacher of youth; but he had, as was affirmed, no pretensions to pulpit eloquence. There was much complaint upon this head among many of the congregation, including a majority of the leading men. The issue was that he resigned. In this affair I saw enough to teach me that the system of appointing the ministers of religion by the suffrages of a society or a congregation is not quite so faultless as has been asserted.

While the people were destitute of a settled pastor the public services were conducted by different ministers. Some of these were students sent from a theological seminary, while others were men who had long exercised the functions of the ministerial office. Among the latter was one whose unusually earnest manner of preaching made a powerful impression upon my feelings. I know not whether he could properly have been called an eloquent man, but he was, unquestionably, both a fluent and impressive speaker; so much so, indeed, as to attract very large congregations whenever or wherever he officiated. His pulpit labours were so effective that it might fairly have been said of him—

"Truth from his lips prevail'd with double sway;
And fools who came to scoff remain'd to pray."

The preaching of this good man moved me far more powerfully than I can well describe. I listened with the deepest interest to his solemn warnings, his earnest expostulations, his forcible delineations of religious character, and his almost graphical descriptions of a future state. It was impossible to suspect him of being otherwise than thoroughly sincere and in earnest; for there was not the slightest symptom at any time of affectation, or any of the other foibles or tricks of a man who, in preaching, was merely acting a part. The interest I felt in hearing his discourses added much to the satisfaction and, I may safely say, to the heartfelt pleasure with which my Sunday pursuits and engagement had for some time been attended. In my earlier years, this day was too often beclouded and made uncomfortable by domestic troubles, which, although I was then so young, I could not witness without much pain and concern; now, however, our affairs were in a little better state, and there was more household comfort. Our Sundays were really seasons of rest and quietness; and, consequently, my amount of enjoyment was much increased. Everything about me on these days seemed to wear a new aspect—that of sacred repose. To me it was a day of inestimable worth. I looked for its return with emotions of heartfelt pleasure, anticipating a day of rational and invigorating enjoyment. Nor was I often disappointed in even the least degree; for though I felt on this day the natural effects of six days' previous and wearying labour, yet I had learned not to be cast down on that account. I, moreover, found my Sunday pursuits and amusements to be powerfully instrumental in cheering and elevating my "inner man." My custom was to have everything I was likely to want on this day got ready for my use on the preceding evening, so that I might have the entire day at my disposal. That I might make the day as long as possible, I rose early: if the mornings were at all fine, I walked in the adjacent fields, where I found ample amusement in either reading the book of nature or some humbler volume, without which I took care *never* to go out on these excursions. About the time that the melodious sound of

"The church-going bells,
The music nighest bordering upon heaven,"

was first heard, I reached home, and there took my frugal meal, in company and converse with my parents and sister. I did this with feelings of satisfaction, such as I wish could be understood by all who are regardless of domestic happiness. After breakfast I sometimes sauntered in my father's little garden, where I either gossiped with him about his flowers and plants, or else indulged in some pleasing reverie, or, in the very idleness of thought, gazed on the " slowly sailing " clouds, or on the quick movements of the birds, or listened to the " pleasing hum" of insects. When less indolent I employed myself in reading. At other times I went out soon after breakfast in order to have a quiet ramble in the spacious, thickly-peopled, and, in my esteem, pleasant graveyard attached to the meeting-house. Here I found much and fitting employment for both the memory and the imagination. I passed by or over the last resting-places of many faded forms, which I remembered to have seen exhibiting the bloom of youth or the vigour of maturity: now the grass, that apt and beautiful emblem of human frailty, flourished on their graves. There were flowers also, which, though wild and generally unregarded, were in my view full of beauty; as they seemed to be emblems, if not pledges, of the resuscitation of the dust over which they diffused a not unpleasing odour. To me they appeared to answer, affirmatively, the anxious question of the querulous patriarch, "If a man die, shall he live again?" Here, then, I read an instructive and an appropriate lesson; one, moreover, which was useful from its tendency to prepare me for the exercises of public worship. I attended on these with becoming seriousness, mingled with much true satisfaction. In these days I rarely thought the service to be either too long or not sufficiently interesting. I was but little concerned about the controversial points of theological doctrine; being principally mindful of what had a direct bearing upon the far weightier matters of practical religion. After the service was over, I sometimes took a short walk, but more frequently returned home immediately, where I spent the interval between the morning and afternoon services much in the same way as I had passed the time at and after my breakfast. In the afternoon I again attended public worship, but a sense of bodily weariness or languor often rendered it less interesting than that of the morning. This eventually led me to question the utility of attending the afternoon service, when that of the morning has not been neglected. My conclusion was in favour of spending the time appropriated to this service in either reading or reflection, or suitable conversation; but this conclusion implied an attendance upon the evening worship. The time between the afternoon and the evening services I always prized very highly. It was, indeed, that part of the Sunday's leisure which I especially enjoyed. The reason for this was, probably, that I then felt much less worn and languid than at any previous hour of the day. This favourable change in my bodily sensations was produced, as I think, partly by the propitious influence of a tranquillized mind upon my very susceptible frame, and partly by my then participating in the refreshing contents of

> "The cups
> That cheer, but not inebriate."

The *repast* known by the name of "*tea*" has *ever been* a favourite one with myself. It is then, if at all, that I feel an increased amount of bodily ease, with more mental activity and enjoyment. I could find it in my heart to bless the memory of him who first brought into notice the shrub which has so often and for so long a time ministered to my comfort. Many a time I have felt greatly revived by merely smelling the odour of the pleasant beverage made from its leaves. I would not exchange this refreshing decoction for any of the productions of the vineyard which I have been allowed to taste, still less for those of the brewhouse or the distillery. These disorder or oppress me, while tea seldom fails to produce the opposite effect of composedness or of exhilaration. Yet I am not hostile—far, indeed, from it—to the temperate use of these stronger drinks; on the contrary, I hold them to be morally lawful, and also useful, on some occasions, to such as have stronger constitutions than mine, or whose avocations require a more powerful stimulant than I can bear.

But I must return to the circumstances and results of my Sunday tea-drinkings. At that repast I usually had a little cheerful conversation with the other members of the household; or else read to them, or listened to what they might read; and thus was agreeably employed until it was time to attend the evening service. This was the more interesting to myself, inasmuch as it was accompanied by a change of scene, on two out of every three occasions. There were three meeting-houses in the town, and this service was performed in each of them successively. One of them was a somewhat time-worn and heavy-looking fabric, having the aspect and character of a by-gone age. The congregation here was usually very small, as the minister—although an excellent man, and of unquestionable ability, as he afterwards showed in the way of authorship—was far from being an "eloquent orator." This paucity of hearers was, however, rather agreeable than otherwise to my feelings; for the place had a much more quiet and suggestive appearance than if it had been better attended. Some of its large, arch-like windows looked out upon a burying-ground belonging to the "Society of Friends." This was a spot that I loved to look at—shut out as it was, and still is, from the public gaze by a rather antique-looking wall, and surrounded, or nearly so, by rows of trees, while the ground itself was covered with beautifully verdant turf. The remains of the worthy people here reposing were laid side by side, in regular order, without any kind of distinction. Here literally the "rich and the poor" met together. One of the windows looked into the garden of an aged clergyman of the Established Church, whom I have occasionally seen in the act of listening to the discourse of his dissenting brother. But there was another window which, in a clear evening, was beautifully illuminated by the soft rays of the setting sun, and to a lively fancy seemed as though it might be one of the portals of that city where all is cloudless and resplendent light.

Of the other two fabrics I shall say but little; they were of more recent date than the one that I have described, and had nothing about them adapted to suggest romantic thoughts or feelings; yet even in these my ever-active fancy would sometimes call up, and then amuse itself with, visions, shadowy and fleeting indeed, yet to me delightful. In one of them I was often pleased with the gentle and graceful waving of some tall poplar-trees, which were visible through the large windows, between which the pulpit was placed: these, together with the windows, the pulpit, and the officiating minister, were not unfrequently irradiated by the chastened light of the declining sun, and then they seemed, in my view, as if a glory from heaven had fallen upon them. These faint outlines or shadowings-forth of the beautiful, when viewed in connection with the exciting spectacle of a large concourse of human beings assembled for the purposes of religious worship, and perhaps just then employed in

"Hymning their Creator's praise,"

were quite sufficient to carry my thoughts far beyond the confines of this "visible diurnal sphere"—to fill my imagination with images of an unseen, yet glorious and beautiful world, and to fill me with ardent desires to become one of its beatified inhabitants. At the close of this service I usually walked in the fields, for the double purpose of recreation and reflection. The day was closed by a slight meal, and I retired to rest with feelings of unalloyed satisfaction. Such were my youthful Sundays, and such also, with but little variation, were those of my riper years, except when I resided in the midst of an overgrown city, or, as subsequently was the case, when the charge of my young children, together with the serious failure of my health, imposed upon me the necessity of spending those invaluable days in a less pleasing, but, I hope, not always in a less appropriate manner. It was about this time (the spring of 1808) that I began to be much concerned as to how I should get a maintenance, should my life be continued. My health was very far from being good; I was troubled with an asthmatic affection, and my strength was unequal to laborious work: hence I was led to perceive the importance of getting an adequate knowledge of the tailoring-trade, which—although I saw it to be a wearying and unhealthy occupation, especially if diligently worked at—I hoped would not be altogether beyond my power. My master had promised that I should learn it, if I could contrive to do so, in the spare hours that might fall to my share. These, however, were very few, seldom more than two or three in the course of a long day; and even these were liable to many drawbacks, as I was frequently taken from my work to run on errands on account of either the house, the drapery-shop, or the tailors. I was much disconcerted and sometimes a good deal discouraged hereat; yet I did not so far despond as to give up my hopes of learning the trade, but resolved upon making a vigorous effort to gain so desirable an end. I therefore immediately set about the business of saving, or rather of making, time for working on the board. Here also, as in my former exertions to get time for reading, I realized the truth of the old proverb, "Where there's a will there's a way;" for being heartily willing, the *way* soon presented itself: this was by working in overhours at my other business. Thus, instead of cleaning the tailor's shop, preparing fuel, and getting the furnace ready in the morning, I did these and other needful things at night, after the men had left off work; by this plan I secured an hour, in the best part of the day, for learning to sew. In addition to this contrivance I also rose yet earlier than before, in order to help one of the workmen, who lived close at hand; I worked with him until it was time to go to the shop, and by this means got both instruction and a little money—sometimes as much as eightpence or tenpence, at the week's end—which was no unimportant addition to the contents of my private purse. Besides these plans, I adopted that of working at home whenever an opportunity offered for so doing; nor did I always allow myself to make a holiday of even the few red-letter-days that fell to my lot; for I well remember having worked on a Good Friday, a beautifully fine day, which seemed almost audibly to invite me into the green and delightful fields. On *that* day I also contrived to amuse myself by committing to memory a large portion of Gray's beautiful 'Ode on Vicissitude.' I further remember to have worked on other holidays—especially on that which, in 1809, was kept in commemoration of the king having entered upon the fiftieth year of his reign.

By dint of persevering industry and attention, aided by the good offices of several of the workmen, I soon got such an insight into the business as enabled me to be very useful upon the board. Ere long my master saw that my services there were more profitable to him than they could be elsewhere; and therefore he consented to hire another, but a younger, boy, to do the greater part of the work which, previously, had chiefly employed my time. I also succeeded in my efforts to get an advance of wages, and thus found myself in a position much more comfortable than that in which I had stood for the preceding three years.

I now had more leisure for reading, and also greater facilities for getting books. Besides these advantages I had that of being able to save a little money for the purchase of clothes and other necessaries. It was at this time that I read the remaining seven volumes of the 'Spectator;' to which I added the 'Rambler,' the 'Tatler,' and some others of the "British Essayists." I also read the poetical works of Milton, Addison, Goldsmith, Gray, Collins, Falconer, Pomfret, Akenside, Mrs. Rowe, with others which I cannot now clearly call to mind. I remember, however, to have read Gay's poems. These gave me more than usual satisfaction. I was much amused with his 'Trivia, or the Art of Walking London Streets;'* but I was especially pleased with

* I have always practically observed the directions implied in the following passages of this amusing composition—I quote from memory:—

"Seek not from 'prentice-boys to learn thy way;
They'll oft deceive and turn thy steps astray—

Ask

his admirably burlesque "pastorals." These just squared with my humour, for I had then, as I have ever had, an utter dislike to the sickening stuff that is *called* pastoral poetry, where one is for ever encountering Daphnes, Delias, and Chloes, Damons and Corydons, with other equally odd or silly personages, who give vent to as many tears, sighs, and groans, as would have sufficed for Milton's imaginary lazarhouse. These fulsome compositions, not excepting those of Virgil,* or the lauded ones of Shenstone, had long been the

"Objects of my implacable disgust."

With these feelings I was not sorry to stumble upon such clever parodies, or rather burlesques, as are those of Gay; they struck me as being clever satires upon productions equally affected and worthless. I must not omit to mention the pleasure I derived from reading a poem called 'The Village Curate,' which, as I think, has fallen into unmerited oblivion.

In the course of my very desultory reading, I perused 'Boswell's Life of Dr. Johnson;' which I still consider to be a very amusing and instructive piece of biography. About this time I read also the narratives of some eminent navigators and travellers; among the former were those of Cook, Pérouse, and Bougainville; of the latter I chiefly remember those

Ask the grave tradesman to direct thee right,
He ne'er deceives but when he profits by 't."
"Who would of Watling-street the dangers share
When the broad pavement of Cheapside is near?"

* I hardly need say that my knowledge of these comes through the medium of a translation.

of Bruce, Le Vaillant, and Weld. Mr. Weld's narrative so deeply interested me, as to have well nigh been the occasion of my emigrating to either the United States or to Canada. The desire of seeing these countries which was excited thereby remained with me for some years: it was the cause of my reading several works descriptive of North America and the condition of its inhabitants.

CHAPTER VI.

In this way I went on until the spring of 1810, when, as I had made myself a fairly competent workman, and moreover, had considerably heated my imagination, by reading and thinking a good deal about London, I resolved to go thither in search of work. My parents, but especially my mother, would fain have dissuaded me from doing this; and I have sometimes wished that I had consented to forego the gratification of my fancy for their sake. Their uneasiness was the greater, because, at that time, two out of their three sons were far from home, and not likely soon to return. I would fain have avoided giving them pain, but I was bent upon seeing the wonderful town, of which I had formed what I soon found to have been a somewhat extravagant notion: I did not, indeed, expect to see houses covered with pancakes instead of tiles; nor to find that the streets were paved either with gold or with penny-loaves; but I did, nevertheless, dream of what I never realized. I had a half-formed notion of getting into society of an intellectual character—somewhat resembling that of which I had read in the 'Spectator,' the 'Rambler,' and other books. I, however, forgot that my purse would not allow me to be a visitor at Will's Coffee House or at the Devil Tavern; that I must, perforce, put up with the accommodations of far humbler places of entertainment, and there be associated with men widely different in character, talents, and learning from Addison, Pope, and Steele, or Burke, Johnson, and Goldsmith. In truth, there was not, at that time, a single place in the metropolis—except the rooms of the Debating Clubs—to which a working man could resort, for the purposes of mental instruction or amusement. Though I had looked forward to my London expedition with very pleasant anticipations, yet, when the time for it came, my courage somewhat failed me. As yet I had never been far from home, nor absent from it for more than two or three days at a time; when therefore I was about to leave both it and my parents, for an indefinite period, I hesitated, and, when called to say "farewell," felt it—for the first time in my experience—to be

" A word that makes us linger."

Since then I have, indeed, pronounced that sadly-sounding word with feelings far more painful than on that occasion, yet I know not that I have ever spoken it with tenderer emotion. But for a foolish dread of

" The world's laugh,
Which scarce the firm philosopher can scorn,"

I should perhaps have declined making the proposed change.

As it was, however, I kept to my purpose, and, becoming amused by the prospects I beheld while travelling, was, by the time I reached the place of my destination, not very "ill at ease." On reviewing the step I had taken, I was, upon the whole, satisfied that it was a proper one. Now, however, I have considerable doubt upon this point. I question whether my real interest was thereby promoted. I probably gained a little additional knowledge of both the "world and the world's ways" by the change; but a wise man has said "He that increaseth knowledge increaseth sorrow," and, so far as my own experience goes upon this matter, I am much disposed to think that he uttered a sober and weighty truth. But let that pass: whether it were for good or for evil, the change was made, nor can its consequences be either altered or obviated:

"What hath been, spite of Jove himself, hath been." *

I must, however, leave these reflections, and go on with my story.

My journey was unattended by any remarkable incident. The country through which I passed is, in general, a level tract, with no features of grandeur or sublimity, and but few that are more than ordi-

---

* Although I quote this line—seeing it answers my purpose—I do not fully approve of the seemingly irreverent manner in which the poet is made to express himself. Where I met with it I cannot well remember, but I think it was in 'A Translation of the Odes, Satires, and Epistles of Horace,' by Mr. Pye, the poet-laureate. I have an old copy of these poems "done into English" by Mr. Creech, in which the sentiment is, I think, much more becomingly expressed. I give it here that the reader may be able to judge between the two renderings:—

"Let Jove to-morrow smiling rise,
Or let dark clouds spread o'er the skies:
He cannot make the pleasures void,
Nor sour the sweets I have enjoyed,
Nor call that back which winged hours have borne away."
Horace, ode xxix., book iii.

narily beautiful. There are, however, some picturesque spots with which I was well pleased, and the more so because to me they had the charm of novelty. I approached London by one of those long-drawn suburban avenues which—like the far-reaching arms of some huge polypus—stretch out their wearisome length from every corner of the metropolis. Here I caught the first glimpse of metropolitan scenes and manners, and I must confess that, although I witnessed much that amused me, I also both saw and heard not a little that was repulsive to my feelings and offensive to my external senses. I say nothing of the "villainous smells" that assailed my olfactory nerves, further than that they formed a striking contrast to the pure and oft-times fragrant air which I had been accustomed to breathe. Yet I must not be severe upon the atmosphere of London —strangely compounded as it is of all sorts of heterogeneous gases—as it certainly then suited my much disordered and over-sensitive lungs, and that to so great an extent as to preserve me from the visitations of my asthmatic complaint.

On entering the "Modern Babylon" I was almost confounded by its "huge uproar," together with the incessant bustle and hurry in which I found myself suddenly involved. My previous notions of London had not, indeed, been quite so erroneous as were those of the Roman peasant in regard to the "Eternal City," yet, although I could not exclaim with him,

> "Fool that I was, I thought Imperial Rome
> Like market-towns (where once a-week we come
> And thither drive our tender lambs from home),"

I certainly did not expect to witness so great a contrast as was here presented to all that I had been accustomed to see in my native place.

I was glad to escape from the hubbub and confusion of the streets, and therefore made the best of my way to my intended lodgings. These were situated in an obscure alley in the neighbourhood of Moorfields, and proved to be almost as quiet a retreat as I could have wished for. In this nook I heard only a subdued and not unpleasing sound, instead of the tumultuous and almost overpowering noise of the crowded and busy thoroughfares. Even at this distance of time I look back upon the many tranquil hours I spent in this humble dwelling with feelings of mingled satisfaction and regret. I yet well remember the vine and the lilac-tree, together with the few flowers that found a place in one corner of the yard, which was dignified with the name of a "garden." It was truly a thriftless spot, yet it had charms for its possessors, as it served to remind them that Nature still lived, and was still arrayed in robes of "sight-refreshing green." And there were persons, also, with whom I here occasionally came into contact who pleased me not a little. Among these was a diminutive and aged woman, who, after having for many years worked in a stove-grate manufactory, had become an itinerant vendor of vegetables and shell-fish. The shrill and plaintive tones in which she announced her commodities—whether they were "*fine Cos lettuce,*" or "*lily-white muscles*"—were, to my ear, far from being unpleasing, indeed they often struck me as being

"Most musical, most melancholy."

MEMOIRS OF A WORKING MAN.

I had two fellow-lodgers, one of whom was a medical student, a man of considerable attainments and of gentlemanly manners, but he was very poor, and nearly if not altogether unbefriended. He was then struggling hard to attain so much anatomical and other professional knowledge as would qualify him to serve in the army, where at that time there was a great demand for the services of medical men. The difficulties and privations that he encountered in prosecuting his purpose were, indeed, sufficient to have dismayed any but the most fearless and determined spirit. They were, in good truth, both numerous and weighty, yet he bore up manfully against them, and ultimately gained his point. Soon after his appointment to the situation of an army hospital mate he was ordered upon foreign service, and set out to join the forces then in Portugal under the command of Sir Arthur Wellesley.

On the day after my arrival in London I went out in quest of employment. This I did in the way which at that time was the most in favour with my fellow-craftsmen, as being thought both more respectable and more profitable than that of waiting upon masters to ask for work. This was by causing my name to be entered in the call-book of a tailors' trade-club, which was held, as all such clubs then were, at a public-house — thence denominated a "house of call." To these houses the masters applied when they wanted workmen. They could here procure, if needful, a fresh supply of men three times per day, viz., at six o'clock in the morning, then at nine o'clock, and again at one o'clock in the afternoon.

The master had the power of discharging a workman at his pleasure, after having given him three hours' work or wages. Thus the men could have as many as three masters in the course of one day.

I was called to work during the very day on which I had my name entered on the call-book, but it was merely for the remainder of that day, as my master was himself a journeyman who wanted a little help about an occasional job of master-work. Here I was, in due form, invested with all the shop-board rights and privileges of the craft, by paying what was technically called my "footing," *i. e.*, in plain English, by treating my workfellows to a fair allowance of porter,—a practice which I subsequently set my face against, and with much success. At night I was discharged, and again repaired to the "house of call," where I received orders to go to work at six o'clock on the following morning for a master residing in Hatton Garden.

I now felt myself at ease. I had fairly launched my tiny bark upon the broad expanse of life's ocean, and I was resolved, if possible, to make a profitable voyage. With this view I applied myself to work with all practicable diligence. It required my utmost efforts to get through the allotted amount of a day's work within the appointed time—for the time as well as the amount of work was strictly regulated. This daily task was considerably too much for any one but a clever and very quick hand, but then, as it was fixed by the workmen themselves, there was neither room for complaining of the masters, nor any good end to be answered by grumbling to the men.

I therefore took the matter quietly, and did my best. This task was, in shop-board phrase, called "the log," and a very appropriate name it truly was, for the task was indeed a heavy one. Yet, as it showed the equitable principles upon which our trade-unions were founded,—in providing that the largest possible amount of labour should be given in exchange for the good wages demanded,—it was generally approved of even by such as, like myself, were not fully equal to the labour it imposed.

When I received my first week's wages, amounting to thirty-three shillings, I was not a little pleased. I felt that I had fairly performed the part of a man, and my self-love prompted me to look upon so meritorious a personage as myself with more respectful feelings than theretofore. My week's wages was a larger sum than I ever before could, at one time, call my own: I was, therefore, comparatively a rich man. Yet, after all, I would gladly have taken three shillings per week less in wages, if thereby I could have escaped from the pressure of that incessant, and to me exhausting toil which I was compelled to undergo, in order to keep up to "the log." My strength, like that of many others, was not equal to this toil,— especially in so hot and otherwise unhealthy a place as is a tailor's workshop, in which I was confined for full twelve hours per day, the hours of working being from six o'clock in the morning until seven o'clock in the evening, one hour only being subtracted for dinner. As to time for breakfast, or any other refreshment, there was not allowed even a moment.

I determined to save some money while work was plentiful, and therefore did not indulge myself much in sight-seeing. Yet I contrived to see something of the metropolitan curiosities in the mornings and evenings of the six working-days, as also on the Sundays: to which were added about two days when I was not wanted by my master. In these scraps of time I caught a glimpse of the principal public buildings, the river, and the shipping; together with the docks and their warehouses. I also ventured upon the expense of paying the accustomed fees in order to gain admission to St. Paul's Cathedral and Westminster Abbey.

I had neither courage nor curiosity sufficient to lead me higher in the ascent of St. Paul's than to the gallery that surrounds the top of the dome. From this point of view, however, I had as extensive a prospect as I could well wish for; but I must confess that it did not give me any great satisfaction. Perhaps I ought to state that I had unfitted myself for pleasure of this sort by the labour of ascending the multitude of stairs leading to this gallery. In addition to the drawback caused by weariness I had no telescope, and, therefore, could see nothing very distinctly of the surrounding country; while what I could see clearly was not much to my taste. I saw no beauty in the confused, shapeless mass beneath me, made up of dirty house-roofs, with their innumerable ranges of "red-hot chimney-pots," together with the spires of churches, and the tall chimneys of the manufactories on the banks of the river. Even this, at the elevation on which I was placed, had lost all its magnificence, and might not inaptly be compared to a silver thread running through a web of dirty sackcloth; or, to a "wounded snake," dragging "its slow length along" between the huge, misshapen piles that overhung, or abutted upon, its banks. Altogether I was less gratified with what I here saw than I had expected to be, and from that day forwards have never felt any wish to look again upon this far-famed panoramic view, unless I could do so with less weariness of body, and with a greater power of distinguishing distant objects.

Of the structure itself I purposely forbear giving an opinion; not only because of my inability to criticise works of art, but also because I suspect myself of having some unreasonable prejudice against the adoption of any other style than that which is commonly called the Gothic, for ecclesiastical edifices. For myself, I greatly prefer the latter style in buildings consecrated to Christian worship, although I am quite willing to believe that the noble edifice referred to is deserving of all the commendation it has ever received from competent judges.

Whatever was the cause, I certainly surveyed the Abbey of Westminster with feelings far more satisfactory and pleasing than were those produced by looking over the Cathedral of St. Paul. The antiquity of this venerable structure; the style of its architecture; the characters and pursuits of the numerous and illustrious persons whose ashes repose under its roof; the variety, expressiveness, and general appropriateness of their sepulchral monuments; together with the almost unbroken stillness of the place, and the quieting influence of the subdued light admitted through its magnificent, storied windows: all these contributed to inspire me with elevating thoughts, and to produce emotions at once solemn and tranquillizing.

But it was during the celebration of divine service that I more especially loved to visit these celebrated places. At these times there was, over and above the emotions usually produced, those which were awakened by the presence of a concourse of people; by the solemn, yet delightful, music of the organ, which to me is the noblest of musical instruments; and by the melodious voices of the choristers.* All these conspired to produce feelings of a most grateful and appropriate order, and seldom failed to call to my remembrance the following beautiful lines of Thomson:—

> "In swarming cities vast,
> Assembled men to the deep organ join
> The long-resounding voice, oft breaking clear
> At solemn pauses through the swelling bass,
> And, as each mingling flame increases each,
> In one united ardour rise to heaven."

---

* I cannot but wish that there was a more full and general use made of the powerful aid of music—both vocal and instrumental—in the celebration of public worship. As to instrumental music, I have long considered the arguments commonly used against its being thus employed to be as nothing when compared with those which may be adduced in its favour. Abstract opinions ought not, as I think, to supersede the authority of facts; and, therefore, I conclude that the undoubted practice of the ancient churches, whether Jewish or Christian, together with a due recognition of the almost miraculous power of music over the human mind, and the almost universal passion of mankind for the delight afforded by this divine art, form a more than sufficient warrant for its constant and ample use in the sacred services of public worship.

In passing, I venture to express a doubt as to the fitness of such edifices as are consecrated to the worship of the "Prince of Peace" for the burying-places of military and naval heroes. These great men doubtless merited all the respect which is shown to their mortal remains; and I am fully willing that their names and deeds should be held in unfading remembrance, and regarded with undiminished honour. Yet I cannot help thinking that these objects would be equally well attained, and that too in a far more appropriate way than now, by depositing their bodies in a public cemetery, or in burying-grounds set apart for the exclusive use of themselves and their humbler companions in arms.

But the Sunday was my most interesting time—my true holiday—when I felt at liberty to go where I pleased, and had no unpleasant thoughts about the loss of time. On this day I usually walked to a considerable distance from my lodging, in order that I might see something new, and also get a view of the country, my relish for which was rather heightened than otherwise by my being, on the other days of the week, debarred from seeing what I so much loved. In the course of these excursions I contrived to visit nearly the whole of the suburban villages, and, in general, was fully repaid for my labour by what I saw, either of Nature's glorious scenes, or of the humbler productions of her handmaid, Art.

While walking to Hampstead, I strayed into a copse not far from my road, where I seated myself upon the trunk of a tree, and read, with no small pleasure, several of the papers contained in that highly entertaining book, 'Sturm's Reflections on the Works of God.' As I read these, surrounded by many of the objects upon which they so pleasingly descant, I was enabled to look "through nature up to nature's God;" to hold, as it were, converse with that glorious and beneficent Being, and to recognize Him as a father and a friend.

I ought to observe that these rambles were not allowed to prevent my regular and timely attendance upon public worship. In my choice of places wherein to join in this delightful service I did not restrict myself to any one sect of professing Christians. Even then I felt it to be impossible to be a party-man. Although I had been brought up among those who dissented from the National Church Establishment, and, moreover, had often heard of its alleged abuses, or defects, I nevertheless frequently joined in its public services with unaffected satisfaction. Notwithstanding whatever I had learned of an unfavourable tendency in regard to the Church and its ministers, I could not help seeing that there was much in the first that deserved my cordial assent, and also, that there were many of the latter who justly claimed my unaffected reverence and esteem. These perceptions were useful to me at the time, and have continued to be so until now. I cannot adequately express the sense I have of the courtesy, the urbanity, and the genuine kindness with which I have been treated by *not a few* of these excellent men, and accomplished gentlemen. But, apart from all personal considerations, I am fully persuaded that the clergy of the Church of England are, as a community, deserving of the most sincere respect, and the fullest confidence of the laity, whether Episcopalians or Dissenters. As to myself, I am not careful about either standards of doctrine, or modes of worship, or rules of discipline. To whichsoever of these diverse matters any one may give the preference is to me quite indifferent; all I wish for is to see a practical attention to the duties which the Christian religion enjoins, and a fair amount of resemblance, in regard to Christian charity, between the professed disciple and his beneficent Master.

But I am wandering wide of my immediate object, and therefore leave this subject, in order to take up the thread of my story. In the course of my attendance on public worship I visited many of the principal churches and chapels in the metropolis and its suburbs, where I heard discourses from the greater number of the preachers who at that time were celebrated for their learning, eloquence, or other pulpit qualifications. I had no restraint upon my movements, for I kept no company with any one. There were, indeed, two or three young men whom I esteemed; but their tastes, or duties, called them into a different path from that in which it was either my wish or my business to walk; consequently, I was left perfectly free to choose for myself. As to choosing companions from among my fellow-workmen, it was wholly out of the question; for, although I took care to be upon civil terms with every one of them, as indeed I was bound to do, yet this was a very different matter from making them my associates when out of the workshop. I respected some of them as fellow-craftsmen and shop-mates, but I knew not one whom I could choose as a friend. Their habits, language, and modes of thinking were alike quite uncongenial with my own, and "how can two," not to mention a greater number, " walk together, except they be agreed?" Thus I was a solitary being; but I was neither an idle nor a melancholy one. I found much occupation, and that too of a pleasant kind, for all the leisure time that I could command. Sometimes, indeed, I wished for more leisure; and, had I not been bent upon "making hay while the sun shone," so that I might be prepared for a "rainy day," I should probably have gratified this wish. As it was, however, I made myself contented during the six working days with such fragments of time as I could pick out of my walks to and from the shop, and from my dinner-hours. The Sundays were, as I have said, wholly my own; and I took care to make the most of them. After all my contrivances I found but little convenience for reading, except on the Sunday. I always kept a book in my pocket, that it might be at hand in case I should find a few spare minutes. In general I managed to read a few pages while going to and from the workshop. This, however, was a somewhat difficult affair, as my path led me through some of the busiest streets and places in the city; and I hardly need say that these are not the most favourable localities for a thoughtful reader, especially if what he chooses to read demands any thing like close attention. It was while standing at a bookstall that I read with the most advantage. I took care to avail myself of this as often, and for as long a time, as possible; and from these out-of-door libraries picked up a few—perhaps a good many—scraps of useful or amusing information. When I fell out of work—which was about the end of July—my first step was to put myself on "short allowance," in order that I might not too rapidly lessen my resources. Perhaps I carried my abstemiousness too far for the due security of health; but the event proved that, in all other respects, my strict parsimony had been a very prudent matter.

CHAPTER VII.

I HAD long felt a great repugnance against what is called "tramping" in quest of work; as I had seen much of the misery consequent thereon in the wretchedly-clad and half-starved persons of many among the numerous "trampers" who had, from time to time, visited my first master's workshop, for the purpose of getting pecuniary relief from the journeymen. I therefore resolved to "keep my standing," even if I did not "take a penny;" being of opinion that, if I must submit to be pinched in regard to food, it would be far easier to bear the said pinching while in a state of comparative repose, than it would be while wandering about the country in vagrant wretchedness.

I now spent my time in walking about the town, in order to see all the curiosities that might be looked at without charge. I was never tired of gazing upon the noble river, with its "forest of masts," and took care to get a view of it from as many different points as I could. On one occasion I took what then seemed the rather adventurous step of crossing the stream. I was on the Isle of Dogs, and, catching from thence a glimpse of Greenwich Hospital, my desire to see this magnificent place to better advantage got the better of my fears, and thus I was induced to commit myself to the care of a jolly waterman, and to the mercy of the broad river. I may just add that I had a full recompense for the perils of the voyage in the amusement I found while looking at the Hospital and its weather-beaten inmates.

In the chapel I was struck by what I thought to be the exquisite beauty of the marble columns that support the organ-gallery; and by the very appropriate subject of the large picture which forms the altar-piece. Of the walk I had in the beautiful park adjacent I will only say, that, for the sake of freely enjoying that privilege in my old age, I seem as if I could persuade myself to encounter the perils of the ocean during my younger years.

Another of my favourite places of resort was the Royal Exchange, with its convenient piazzas. Under these I spent many a tranquil hour, although in the immediate neighbourhood of thronged and busy thoroughfares. I found a good deal of amusement in running over the numerous and greatly diverse articles which were there advertised for sale or hire in placards of equal diversity. I sometimes remained during 'Change time, when the foreign merchants, some of whom wore their national costume, led my imagination into distant lands, among strange scenes and yet stranger people, among which it wandered until the bell of the porter announcing the close of the business hours awoke it from its pleasing dreams. The time passed away pleasantly for about a fortnight, when, as I was sauntering along Fleet Street, my attention was arrested by a large map of my native county. I surveyed it with composure until I came to the mark that showed the situation of the town from whence I came, upon which I was attacked by that very powerful disorder of the fancy called the "home-sickness." This continued to grow upon me until it threatened to be incurable except by the influence of the objects whose shadows had been the means of producing it. In this predicament I was not long in determining what to do. My little affairs were immediately settled; I left the metropolis, with all its attractions, and soon found myself once more at home.

It was autumn, which, as I have already stated, has ever been to me the most delightful and congenial of all the seasons. It was at this time the more welcome because of my having previously been a good deal shut up in places where the atmosphere was unwholesome, and the prospect, if there were any, far from being a pleasant one. I now, however, could " breathe and walk again" in and among fresher and fairer scenes.

When at home I usually retired to my garret, where I employed myself in either reading or working. It was truly a humble and homely apartment, but it was in my view a very pleasant nook. In reading I usually sat in the Oriental, or, to use a less pompous word, in the tailor's posture, and thus had no need of either chair or table. My olfactory nerves meanwhile were regaled by the smell of sundry roots and herbs which were stowed in this room for the purpose of being properly preserved for future use. Among these the onion had a prominent if not a pre-eminent place, to my great satisfaction, for it was one of my favourite roots in regard both to its flavour and odour. I was rarely idle, for when tired of reading I fell to tailoring, having long before that time learned that

"Absence of occupation is not rest,"

but rather a source of almost intolerable weariness.

The books I read at this time related chiefly to North America. Among the chief of them were Ramsay's 'History of the American Revolution,' Smith's 'Travels in Canada and the United States,' and Parkinson's 'Travels in North America.'

The tailoring work to which I have referred being finished, I tried to procure regular work at some one of the shops in the town. I succeeded, however, but very indifferently, because it was then the season of the year in which cucumbers are said to be vended at the rate of two for a penny, when, according to the averment of the Covent-Garden-Market ladies, "tailors, twice as many," may be had for the like sum. In this dilemma I resolved, for once, to break my rule as regarded "tramping," and accordingly walked to a town about sixteen miles distant in search of employment. My journey was bootless in respect of its main object, yet I did not think that the time spent in it was thrown away, inasmuch as I saw a good deal of what gave me pleasure, although it was neither grand, novel, nor eminently beautiful. There was, however, much that I thought to partake of that character which is called "picturesque," and therefore I could not fail to be amused, for I have always loved to look at either a similar landscape or at whatever fairly represents it.

On my way homeward I discovered that I had overrated my physical ability when I undertook a walk of more than thirty-two miles in one day, in weather rather warmer than common. Before I had got more than four miles on my journey I became very ill, and was quite unable to proceed. In this dilemma I contrived to reach a neighbouring alehouse, where I hoped to get some rest, for I was much worn by fatigue. The landlady was a kind-hearted woman, and therefore freely accommodated me with a bed, not regarding the danger there might be of my becoming both a troublesome and an unprofitable inmate. After getting two or three hours' repose, I was so far refreshed as to warrant my attempting to prosecute my journey. I thankfully as well as cheerfully paid the charge made by my hostess, amounting to about threepence, and again turned my steps towards home, where I arrived in a better plight than I could have expected.

When I had spent about seven weeks with my parents, I was disturbed by the preparations then making for balloting men to serve in the militia. I deprecated the life of a soldier, and this on several accounts. Among these was the conscientious objection I felt to war in the abstract, and the pain I endured on witnessing, as I often had, the direful effects of warlike operations, even when my own countrymen were the victorious combatants. I was moreover unfit to be the bearer of arms, as I had neither bodily strength nor "martial build" sufficient to carry me through the hardships of even a militiaman's duty, besides which my disposition, tastes, and habits were such as to fill me with dislike for the noise and fatigue, the turbulence and the restlessness, of a military occupation. It was therefore but natural that I should look for some loophole through which to escape the perils of the ballot. On doing this I discovered one which seemed likely to answer my purpose. As I had long been afflicted by spasmodic asthma, I concluded that I had sufficient ground of exemption from military service. Great therefore was my surprise, when, on applying for a medical certificate of my unfitness for this service, I was refused one, although the gentleman to whom I applied knew something of my physical state, and moreover told me that he thought I was inadequate to a soldier's duties. This refusal made me resolve to change my residence before the coming of the balloting-day. I therefore again left my parents, and sought a home in London, where I hoped to be secure from further molestation about soldiership, and all other matters connected therewith. Herein I was not disappointed, for I had no trouble on these accounts so long as I remained in the metropolis.

On my revisiting London I took lodgings in the same house, and thus far I was tolerably at home. Trade, however, continued to be very dull, so that I could not procure employment except a few trifling jobs on my own account. Thus I had more than enough time for my other purposes. In good truth, I had much more than I desired to have, or than was at all consistent with my well-being, yet as there was no help for it, I endeavoured to be contented. I employed the greater part of it in reading and walking; and in order to see as much as I could I varied my walks; but my favourite haunts were, as before, the

Royal Exchange, and the banks of the river below London Bridge. Sometimes I rambled westward, and then I rarely omitted visiting Westminster Abbey for the purpose of seeing the various interesting objects in Poets' Corner. I did not then know of the Cloisters, or I should have availed myself of the facility they afford for a quiet walk. There was free access given to that part of the Abbey which I have named, otherwise my visits there would have been both " few and far between." As it was, however, I put no check upon my wishes, but often spent an hour or two in quietly contemplating the monuments which either public esteem or private affection had there placed in memory of departed genius, learning, or moral worth. It is a place in which, as it seems to me, there may be learned much both of an admonitory and an encouraging character, in which there are numerous and affecting intimations concerning the " vanity of human wishes," and the utter insignificance of all that men deem " good or great," unless it be connected with the practice of moral virtue, and therefore bearing upon the interests of another and a nobler life.

In these western rambles I sometimes looked into the courts of law and equity. In the latter I had one day an opportunity of hearing several long and dry harangues respecting some houses which were claimed by different parties. I was amused by the seeming inattention of the Lord Chancellor (Eldon), as I also was by the contrast between his sombre habiliments and the parchment-like hue of his face. When, however, it came to his turn to speak, I was much surprised by his clear recapitulation of what had been said—stripping it of all its verbosity and tautology; and I was so much pleased by hearing his earnest deprecation of a Chancery suit in the case before him, that I ever afterwards felt a high respect for his Lordship, as being an *equitable* as well as an *equity* judge.

I have noticed more than once my predilection for visiting the Royal Exchange. My chosen time for these visits was that between the hours of ten and one o'clock, during which hours the piazzas were but thinly attended, while the great area of the place was wholly unoccupied. Here, as I have already partly hinted, I found a comparatively quiet spot, to which I was for the time glad to retreat, in order that I might get out of the incessant bustle and the stunning confusion of the crowded streets, which sometimes were more than I could endure without a sense of pain and weariness.

Some one has said that "a great city is a great solitude," and such I found London to be, notwithstanding the vast stream of human beings which filled and almost overflowed its public ways,

"From early morn to evening's latest hour."

Many a time have I wandered through most of the principal streets and other thoroughfares without seeing even one person whom I could recognise, much less any of "the old familiar faces," the sight of which is so pleasant an ingredient in the cup of life to one whose lot is cast among strangers. Thus, in the capital of my native country, I have sometimes felt almost as lonesome and friendless as were the natives of China or Hindostan, many of whom were at that time to be found in the avenues of the metropolis.

This sense of loneliness was frequently accompanied by feelings of vexation on witnessing the indifference of the strong and active passengers to either the safety or the convenience of such as were less robust and vigorous than themselves. I have often seen pain inflicted upon the sickly and the infirm by those who seemed to be strangers to pain, and moreover strangers to that sympathy with suffering humanity which constitutes so fine a part of man's moral nature, and which a personal knowledge of affliction is adapted to call into action. In most of these cases there was probably no intention of doing wrong, yet the wrong was done, and that too without any expression of regret on the part of the doer. This it was that provoked me, as being indicative not so much of thoughtlessness as of heartless selfishness. The injured person was left without even the poor recompense of an apology. It seemed to be the offender's only care to get away as quickly as possible, in order thereby to avoid a claim upon his purse, or lest he should miss the object upon which his heart appeared to be so earnestly set that he was impelled to pursue it at all risks. Whatever this object was, it was pursued with as much eagerness as if the fate of a universe had been depending upon its attainment.

While I was angry at incidents like these, I was often a witness of such as affected me with mournful feelings. I could not look upon the many wretched-looking people whom I everywhere saw without commiserating their destitute condition; and this feeling was the more painful because of my inability to give them any efficient help. I refer not here to the class of sturdy and clamorous mendicants whose well-conditioned although ragged and dirty persons gave the lie to all their melancholy tales of impending starvation, but to the hapless beings who moved silently along, "with faltering steps and slow," bearing upon their faces the marks of hopeless grief, and exhibiting in their much-worn yet decent attire the signs of their having formerly seen better days. Such desolate people as these may at any time be seen in the streets of London by him who takes only the small trouble of looking about him with an observant eye. They clamour not for relief; but while famine and cold and sorrow are performing their work of desolation upon them, they bear their heavy load without obtruding themselves upon the notice of the passers-by. I have looked at such evidently famishing persons with feelings of deep sympathy on their account, mingled, at times, with the melancholy thought that a similarly destitute state might one day be mine.

It was on accounts like these that I sometimes felt no pleasure in perambulating the high-ways—much less the *by-ways*—of the metropolis; and would gladly have escaped for awhile into some less beaten and more tranquil paths than those in which there were so many saddening spectacles; and where, moreover, the

"Ever-moving myriads seem'd to say,
'Go—thou art nought to us, nor we to thee—away.'"

Yet there were times in which these feelings were not so fully awakened, and when, therefore, I could find both amusement and acceptable instruction in these much-thronged avenues. At these seasons they seemed to present an open book, upon whose broad and diversified pages, even he who ran might see inscribed many an instructive lesson of practical knowledge. I need not say that these lessons were not all of the same import. Some were animating or encouraging; others were simply prudential; while others were expressive of earnest admonition or of solemn warning. All of them, however, were powerfully impressive, because they were *living* lessons made up of the combined aspects, sayings, doings, and states of sentient beings—of men, women, and children— almost without number, and derived from almost every region of the inhabited earth — a vast and widely-varied multitude, drawn together by that powerful and ever-working impulse, which, in all times and places, leads man to seek the society of his fellow-man. For myself, I was both an earnest and an unwearied reader of these "living epistles:" but with what success I venture not to say. I may, however, safely affirm that if they failed to instruct me, they did not fail to afford me much harmless amusement.

I now turn to subjects upon which I hope to be less querulous than in some of the preceding remarks. I was at this time amusing myself with some daydreams about emigrating to the United States of America; but, while thus engaged, I did not forget matters nearer home and of more immediate interest.

I therefore continued daily to look out for work, but still without success. This gave me considerable uneasiness, and the greater because my stock of money was by this time a good deal reduced. To meet this exigence, I still further reduced my expenditure; so that my charges for living were about as low as those of an inmate of a poor-house. It may not be amiss to present the reader with my usual bill of fare. The account for one day will suffice, as I allowed of no high-days or holidays. Even the slightest expense that was not indispensably needful, was carefully avoided. For breakfast I had a penny roll and half a pint of porter. This I took at a publichouse—for two reasons: first, that I might have an opportunity of looking at the morning newspaper; and further, that I might have the comfort of sitting by a good fire—for the wintry season was not far off, and the mornings were already cold. As an impartial and faithful narrator, I am bound to confess that this meal cost me a *halfpenny* more than the sum charged for the provisions, because I preferred the accommodations of a room where I could sit quietly, and without the annoyance of tobacco-fumes. For this privilege I willingly incurred the additional expense, and thus spent many an hour in tolerable comfort, which otherwise must have been spent either in the cold and cheerless streets, or among the noisy and uncouth frequenters of a dirty tap-room. I felt a considerable degree of interest in regard to the course of public affairs, and therefore was the more anxious to see a newspaper every day. I also hoped that some one of the numerous advertisements might be made available in the way of getting employment other than that of tailoring. In this hope I was disappointed; yet the time I thus spent was not quite thrown away, as I hereby contracted a habit of carefully reading advertisements, which I have found to be useful. So fixed and powerful is this habit, that I never omit looking over the advertising columns of every newspaper that comes fairly within my reach, and I often do this at the expense of leaving unread all its other contents. It may be a merely fanciful notion on my part, but I nevertheless seem to learn more of human nature and of the tangled web of human affairs from these sources than I am able to learn from the most laboured statements of either editors or paid correspondents. While these, in order to bring grist to the mill, are forced to comply with party views and to suppress their own; or are induced to mystify plain questions, so that they may seem to be profoundly learned in political knowledge; the advertising parties write for themselves—throw aside the veil of mystery—ask in good plain English for the reader's cash, and generally give a fair view of what is going on in the regions of their inner man. There are, indeed, some cases in which the advertisers employ a few cabalistical phrases in their announcements; but these may be soon interpreted. When *this* is done, the reader will not fail to discover what may, perhaps, help to guard him from becoming a victim to the cupidity, trickery, or base selfishness which may often be partially concealed under cover of very plausible statements. But I am neglecting my bill of fare, in like manner as I then sometimes

G

neglected to get my dinner—that is to say, by having my thoughts fully occupied about other matters. I have but a very slender account to give of my noonday meal, inasmuch as I frequently dined in the style of "Duke Humphrey," and in a similar place. When I did have a dinner, it was made out of a penny loaf unaccompanied by the addition of anything besides. Of the meal usually called "tea," I say nothing, and for a good reason, namely, that I really have nothing to say, inasmuch as it had no place among my meals. In consideration of my abstinence during the day, I venture to hope for the reader's verdict in respect of my rather plentiful supper. At this meal I allowed myself a sufficient quantity of food; but as to its quality I cannot say much in its favour. It consisted of bread and cheese, porter, and onions—food which I have always much relished, but which was, even then, far too crude and heavy for my feeble digestive powers. It was, however, very palatable, and considerably the more so because of my having had the appetite a good deal sharpened by much previous abstinence, and by exposure to a cold atmosphere. After all, however, it was not the food merely that made this meal so acceptable. I was fully as much gratified with the opportunity it gave me of reposing myself in an easy chair by the side of a good fire, and also of having a little pleasant chat with my host and hostess, together with my fellow-lodger; and I yet further valued this hour, because of its affording me a better convenience for reading than I could command during the day. Besides all which, it was the *evening-time,* and I then, as I ever have done, preferred *this* far before every other. I am not insensible to the cheerful influence of the morning—whether it be that of the natural day, or year, or of the day of human life; but the morning is the season of hopes that may, perhaps, be disappointed—of purposes that may be broken off—of wishes that may never be gratified—and of innumerable pleasing but nameless emotions, which, in all probability, will meet with no kindred response.* All these hazards and uncertainties make the morning to me a time rather of pensive thought than of gladsome feeling, whereas the evening speaks of the past; and although in *that* past there may have been much upon which we desire not to look again, yet there is the consolation of knowing that

" The past temptations
No more shall vex us "—

---

* I here give a verse or two of a poem which—considering what is stated in the text—the reader will not wonder that I should have retained in the memory, although nearly forty years have gone over me since I read it:—

" Youth's rosy morn, serenely glowing,
    Impearls the buoyant spray;
The sparkling tides of pleasure flowing,
Where fancied tufts of flow'rets blowing,
    Their mossy banks inlay.
Life throbs alert, ah! little knowing
    How sets its day.

Dark skies, with tempests intersected,
    Man's fiercer noon invest;
Plans cross'd—hopes thwarted—love neglected—
Wounds from the objects least suspected—
    Unnerve his iron breast.
The cheat, alas! too late detected,
    Too long caress'd."

that the perils and toils, the cares and griefs, of the day are gone, and gone for ever.

Thus, at the hour of evening, I have always been ready to exclaim with him of whom Thomson says that

"He never utter'd word, save—when first shone
The glittering star of eve—'Thank Heaven! the day is done.'"

Or with him who, speaking in his own person and from the impulse of deep and unaffected emotion, thus addresses this delightful visitant:—

"Come, evening, once again, season of peace;
Return, sweet evening, and continue long!
 . . . . . .
I slight thee not, but make thee welcome still."

So welcome, indeed, was she, that I seldom contemplated her departure without somewhat of a painful feeling; and when she was forced to go, I often endeavoured to make up her loss by giving such entertainment as I could to Night, her twin-sister, and who is said to be

"Fair Virtue's immemorial friend."

I have had some experience of the salutary and benignant influence of this "sable goddess," and must not omit to record my grateful remembrances of the many benefits and pleasures I have derived from her society. Even while I write I go back to these hallowed interviews, and again say, as I have often said in the spirited language of him who was especially her poet and eulogist,

"Hail, precious moments!—stolen from the black waste
Of murder'd time; auspicious midnight, hail!"

But for these moments—which in my case were indeed snatched from the wrecks of time—I should never have enjoyed the privilege of holding converse with many among the illustrious dead, who still live in their imperishable works. It may have been that my reading at these unseasonable hours had an unpropitious effect upon my bodily health; of this, however, I am not sure, and if I were so, I should be very unlikely to regret the issue, for I still think that a portion of physical vigour given for that which conduces to the amelioration of the mental state, is neither an ill-judged nor a profitless exchange. I now turn from these speculations to a matter of fact, which, although very trifling in itself, gave me much vexation and some anxiety. It so happened that I made a serious inroad upon my poorly-stocked purse by a foolish transaction, of which I soon repented, but, as is often the case in concerns of greater moment, without avail, except that I learned to be thenceforward more cautious in buying what I did not want. I fancied that a pair of boots would improve my personal appearance, which, to speak the truth, was really in want of some amendment, inasmuch as both my dress and gait were considerably out of the fashion. Urged on by this fancy, I ventured to bespeak a new pair of what were called Hessian boots, nothing doubting that my outward man would be greatly embellished by having the legs encased in a pair of these fashionable habiliments. The result proved that I had "reckoned without my host," for it turned out that the worthy son of Crispin to whom I gave the order was incompetent to the task I had set him. When the boots made their appearance, I discovered that I had made a sad mistake as to their maker's knowledge of the fashion, and at once perceived that, if I wore them, they would give me a yet more uncouth appearance than that which I so much wished to lay aside. As to the materials and workmanship I believe there was no fault to be found; but in regard to shape, they were so odd and out-of-the-way, that I verily think they could not have been easily matched, even among the enormous boot-stores of the Great Metropolis. They were, in short, well worthy of a niche in some museum of outlandish costumes. Thus I was doubly mortified, for I not only found myself minus in the good round sum of thirty-six shillings, but also was saddled with an article in exchange for which I felt that I had neither taste nor use. Yet, as there was no remedy, I put the best face I could upon the matter, wore the unfortunate boots, and consoled myself with the thought that I would in future be more careful in regard both to the choice of a craftsman and spending money for unnecessary articles. For some time, however, I was a good deal troubled about this affair, as I rather dreaded its consequences would be a realization of that shrewd proverb in Poor Richard's Almanac, "He that buys what he has no occasion for, will soon be forced to sell his necessaries." Yet, after all, it did not turn out so bad as I had foreboded, although it made a still further reduction of my necessary expenses an immediate duty. By dint of hard living I made my cash hold out until I procured work, at which time, however, it was nearly all expended.

CHAPTER VIII.

I FOUND employment sooner than I should have done, in consequence of a death in the Royal Family. It was that of the youngest daughter of the reigning monarch. This event caused a sudden demand for black clothes, it being the custom on these occasions for a public mourning to be ordered, which continued altogether for several months. At this time there was a great stir for two or three weeks among the tailors, which of course was soon followed by a general stagnation of the tailoring trade,* to the great injury of multitudes belonging to the craft. With a view to lessen this, it had been the rule—founded, as it was said, upon a law—to allow double wages to the workmen for a month from the day of a royal person's decease. But this humane provision was made the occasion of much contention and ill-will. First, there were disputes between the master-tailors and many of their customers on account of the increased charges for clothes; and, consequently, there

* The cause of this will be readily seen, if it be remembered that, for so long as the mourning continued, there was but very little demand for any but black clothes. The mischief was increased by the facility with which these can be scoured and otherwise improved, so as to make them look well for a much longer time than is possible in regard to clothes of any other colour. This is especially the case in the winter season—the time in which this incident occurred.

was a good deal of bickering about wages between these masters and their journeymen. After many struggles the masters so far succeeded as to get rid of the double wages, except for *black* clothes only. At the next public mourning they further objected to the extra payment even for *black* clothes, except they were ordered solely on that account. By this time, therefore, the privilege of having double wages on these emergencies was greatly reduced in value. The master who now gave me work expressly stipulated that I should receive only single wages for whatever garments I might make. To this I was forced to consent, or incur the danger of being for a still longer time out of employment. Thus situated, I went to work with a determination to make the " best of a hard bargain," and succeeded tolerably well in my efforts.

I continued to work for this master until trade became so dull that he was obliged to discharge several of his workmen, among whom I was included. I was glad to find that I had given him satisfaction, for he promised to employ me again so soon as his business became more brisk. It was, however, more than two months before he had an opportunity of redeeming this pledge; during which time, notwithstanding that I had saved a little money while at work, I should certainly have suffered considerable inconvenience but for the good offices of a fellow-workman. This friendly man was able to procure work from a wholesale clothing-house in the City. He did this whenever his usual supply failed him; and on this occasion he took out as much as sufficed to keep both of us busily employed. Thus, during four or five weeks of the dreary midwinter I was busy at work, and, moreover, as comfortable as I could reasonably wish to be. I worked in the same room with my friend, and therefore had the advantage of being both warmer and at less cost than if I had worked alone. He charged me nothing for either shopboard-room, fire, or candles, and, moreover, allowed me several little accommodations which added considerably to my comfort while at work. I have long ago forgotten his name; but I hope never to forget his disinterested kindness. The work I was employed about consisted chiefly of garments for the East India Company's naval and military officers. They were wanted in time to be forwarded to India by one of the ships belonging to the Company's March fleet. When they were all made my friend's power to help me was at an end, as he had no more work than was needful for his own purposes, and thus I was again left without employment. This, however, now gave me but little concern, as the spring-time was approaching, and I felt assured would bring with it a revival of business. What anxiety I did feel was speedily relieved by my being sent for by my former master. Here I was again provided for, and moreover was as comfortably situated as I could wish, being on good terms with both my master and my fellow-workmen; while my earnings were good enough to allow of my again saving a little money. I here saw another example, in addition to several that I had previously witnessed, of the evil effects produced upon apprentices by their being allowed to eat and drink without restraint. The consequence of this full feeding was in each case such an indolent and careless habit as effectually prevented the lad from learning to be either a quick or a clever workman. In this case the youth was of good moral character, and also of very agreeable manners, but he was too well fed to allow of his feeling able to work properly. When, therefore, his apprenticeship had expired, he was incompetent to be a journeyman, and soon descended to the very humble station of a tailor's trotter.*

There is a proverb current among our craft, which says that " A half-starved tailor works the best ;" and if this be understood as simply meaning that a temperate man is the best fitted for effective labour, I fully subscribe to its truth. I hesitate not to say, that while I have seen many instances of the bad consequences of full feeding among my fellow-workmen, I have never seen one of an opposite character. At the hazard of incurring the warm displeasure of some who may read this, I must now write that which I have often said with the living voice.

It may seem harsh, but it is not the less true, that tailors, in general, are both improvident and intemperate men. They have, I know, many temptations to both these faults; but this is no valid excuse. In proportion to the force of the temptations ought to

* A tailor's trotter is one whose business it is to wait on the master and his workmen in various ways—such as to clean out the cutting-room and the workshop, to see that the men are duly provided with hot irons (for pressing their work), to get what they may want out of the cutting-room, to brush and carry home clothes, &c. In short, he is a " servant of all work."

be their efforts to resist them. By doing this, they would get rid both of their ill-name, and also of much personal suffering. I always held these views, as many among them can testify, and I have sometimes been glad to see that my efforts to enforce them have not been without some good effect. One of the men with whom I was now working was a striking example of their truth and value. He was, indeed, a pattern of industry, prudence, and temperance. May I give a brief sketch of this worthy man? His name betokened his relationship to the "Emerald Isle," being none other than "Patrick Crawley." By dint of persevering attention to the virtues just named, Patrick, helped by his good wife, had contrived to become the tenant of a good house and the master of a flourishing business in the earthenware line, in the fashionable town of Brighton. When the tailoring trade was brisk in London, he left his house and business under the care of his wife, while he went thither to look after work. As at these times there was an increased demand for workmen, he did not often long want a master. When he had found one, he was not likely to be soon discharged, because his working abilities, as also his general appearance and deportment, were such as made him a valuable workman. We soon became good friends, as well as friendly shop-mates. It may not be amiss to remark that he was a member of the Roman Catholic Church, while I was a Protestant, and moreover a dissenter from the National Church establishment; but this difference of religious profession made no difficulty in the way of our maintaining mutual good-will. All that we found needful was a little mutual forbearance, and as we agreed to exercise this towards each other's religious scruples, we went on very smoothly; nor do I believe that any dispute would ever have arisen between us on these grounds. I will just add here that I have never found any difficulty whatever in regard to living at peace with members of the Roman Catholic Church (of whom there were *very many* among my numerous shop-mates during twenty years). Nor have I ever concealed or given up any part of my religious opinions in order to conciliate these men; on the contrary, I have always avowed my attachment to the Protestant faith. All that I ever found needful in order to preserve a friendly feeling, has been a proper regard to their feelings, both as men and as the zealous members of a church which, despite of its errors or defects, I saw to be the instrument of much good, both private and public. I am bound to say that I have ever found the consistent members of the Romish Church to be far better men, in every respect, than were the avowed sceptics and practical atheists, which so much abounded among the *nominal* Protestants of the shop-board.

When the spring-trade had fully set in, my Hibernian friend thought it would be more advantageous to connect himself with a house-of-call. In this opinion I agreed with him, and consequently we lost no time in carrying our views into effect. By this arrangement, however, we ceased to be fellow-workmen, for we were called to work by different masters, so that our future intercourse was merely occasional. In the course of a few months it ceased altogether, by reason of our leaving London, and taking up our residence in towns far removed from each other.

About this time I went upon what I am forced to call "a foolish errand," because I had repeatedly seen, although on a smaller scale, what I went to gaze at. This was nothing less than a grand military review, which was about to be held on Wimbledon Common. The weather was hot; the road was dusty, and thronged with carriages of all sorts, as well as by an almost overwhelming number of people. Yet, for myself, I certainly had no business to be among them. The review was a very magnificent affair; quite as splendid, perhaps, as a show of that kind could well be. The troops were numerous, well clothed, and completely equipped. They were reviewed by the Prince of Wales, accompanied by his brothers the Dukes of York and Cumberland, together with the nominal King of France (Louis XVIII.) and several other male branches of the French royal family, which at that time was enjoying a comfortable asylum in England, while the great Napoleon was riding rough-shod over not only France, but also over nearly every other kingdom of Europe. The spectators were truly multitudinous, and when they lifted up their united voices in one general acclamation, might have reminded one of that yet more numerous assemblage which

"Up sent
A shout that tore hell's concave;"

or rather, of that whose combined voices are represented as resembling the noise of "mighty thundering," or of "many waters."

On my return homewards I became very ill, through fatigue and involuntary fasting; I say involuntary, because I really could not procure suitable refreshments either on or near the ground, as the supply of eatables and drinkables was not equal to the demand. I at length reached an ale-house, where I found both rest and provisions, and thus in a short time was enabled to resume my walk.

In due time I reached home, when, as was my usual custom, I sat in judgment upon the proceedings of the day. As I reviewed these with some degree of coolness and impartiality, I found that I had been guilty of indiscretion; for which I regarded my fatigue and loss of cash as no more than a just correction. I could not balance the account—as between debtor and creditor—without perceiving that I had been concerned in a profitless transaction; while if I looked at it solely in the light of a necessary charge for amusement, I felt that I had paid a great deal " too much for my whistle."

The upshot of the whole matter was, that I resolved to be more cautious in future as regarded running after either military or any other merely showy exhibitions—a resolution which I have tolerably well kept from that time until now.

Ere I leave this subject, I wish to observe that I do not wholly decry military spectacles, nor do I include others in the censure which I have just passed upon myself:—

" Different minds
Incline to different objects;"

and even the same mind at different seasons or stages

of life is not affected in the same way by the same objects or incidents. Thus, as all have their peculiar tastes, and as there is said to be no disputing, with certainty, about these, it may be that there is some real beauty or grandeur in scenes of " martial pomp and array," although I may not *now* be able to discover wherein it lies; otherwise it is hard to account for the intense interest they create in so many minds, which, nevertheless, are neither puerile nor untaught; an interest, moreover, which is as enduring as it is powerful.

It was also about this time that I acted unwisely in another instance. Herein I exposed both myself and others to considerable danger. It was through reading in bed by candlelight without taking due care to guard against accident by fire. Being very weary, after a long day's work, and yet anxious to read a little before I slept, I endeavoured to do this in a way that might answer the double purpose of getting some physical rest and amusing myself: I therefore placed the candle upon my pillow, and assumed a reclined posture, forgetting that, by doing this, I was rather inviting sleep than preparing myself for intellectual exertion. Ere long the fatigued body asserted its claim to entire repose, and I fell into a sleep from which I did not awake until my candle was much wasted. It was still burning, and moreover was close to my head; while the scattered state of my books showed that I had moved enough while asleep to have incurred considerable danger.

But for the goodness of Him who " neither slumbers nor sleeps," the issue of this seemingly trifling incident would, probably, have been calamitous to many, and fatal to more than one; as the house in which I lodged, together with those adjoining it, was old, dry, and crowded with inhabitants.

Sometimes I took a walk in the evening, and then I occasionally found my way into a bookseller's shop, the keeper of which sold books by auction nearly every evening. The books offered for sale were chiefly of but little value. There was sometimes a useful book, but as this commonly found a goodly number of bidders, and therefore was sold at a rather high price, I was seldom a purchaser. Thus, in general, I was only a spectator of what I found to be a not unamusing scene. Among other matters, I noticed that it often happened, when the auctioneer came to a *saleable* lot, his assistant could not find it, upon which the next lot was called for without delay. The frequency of this accident made me suspect that it was not altogether what it seemed to be.

At one of these sales I bought a copy of ' Bloomfield's Poems,' but not so cheaply as to encourage me to continue my biddings. I read Bloomfield with much interest, as I also did a copy of Montgomery's ' Wanderer in Switzerland, and other Poems.' Being at the time in poor health of body, at which times my imaginative faculty has always been morbidly active, I was unwise to read poetry of this class, which, under the circumstances, was more likely to excite uneasy feelings than to invigorate the mind. And thus it fell out; for while I read of rural scenes, and also of the comparative quietude and the superior happiness of a country life, I grew weary and heart-sick of the noisy and restless town, although that town was no less than the " resort and mart of all the earth ;" and forthwith so earnestly wished once more

" To gaze at Nature in her green array,"

as led me to resolve upon again changing the place of my abode. To one in my circumstances this was no difficult matter. I therefore was soon ready to bid, what I intended to be a final, adieu to London, and ere long was snugly quartered in my father's cottage.

My first care was to seek employment, which I soon found, because, in addition to trade being brisk, I was considered to be a competent workman, inasmuch as I had been working in London, which was thought to be the only efficient school for juvenile tailors.

My new master was, in many respects, a remarkable man. Without anything more than a brief, and necessarily imperfect, training, he was metamorphosed from what he previously was, into a working tailor, and from this he quickly graduated to the rank of a master. Several circumstances just then combining to make a fair opening for another master tradesman in that line, he adroitly and seasonably availed himself of them, and following up the advantages of his position, soon found himself to be the chief tailor in the town and its vicinity. For many years he carried on a very extensive tailoring business — working very generally, and with much repute, for the numerous military officers successively quartered in the district, which comprised several garrisons. He also contracted largely for clothing entire regiments ; besides which, he was both a wool-merchant and a wholesale woollen-draper. Having, as I have said, obtained what was necessary to my physical support, I endeavoured to make provision for wants of an intellectual kind; I naturally turned to my old and chosen resource, that of books. It had, perhaps, been better for my bodily health, if I had been able to get more out-of-door exercise than can fairly be obtained by one who is called to earn his daily bread by his daily labour at a sedentary business. Without being positively ill, I was so much disordered in body as, for the time, to feel incompetent to the proper discharge of my necessary duties; I felt languid, and wished for some retreat where I might enjoy unbroken rest and quietness. Such a lot as this was, of course, wholly unattainable by such a one as myself, and I *now* think it was well that it was so; for, could I have then compassed it, I think it would have proved but a vain refuge, and that neither the mind nor the body would have received much benefit from its supposed advantages. I have, since then, had some considerable experience in regard both to mental inquietude and bodily disorder; and the result has been a sober conviction that daily and imperative duties, such as call for the vigorous exercise of the mental powers, are among the best alleviations of either trouble or disease. But for the ceaseless pressure of manifold and anxious cares on the behalf of others, I had not borne the burden of personal disorder and infirmity nearly so well as I have done; the mind would have been chained down either to a continual sympathy with the sufferings of the disordered body, or to moody musings upon its own ailments. Yet, although I deprecate complete retirement in a case of this sort, I do not think that a tailor's workshop is a place well adapted to the state of an invalid: its atmosphere is ill suited to preserve, much less to restore, the vigour of the bodily frame; while its society is equally inimical to the health of both the mind and the heart. Such, however, was the scene, and such were the associates, with which I was compelled to be daily and hourly familiar; I need not say that I found both the one and the other to be not a little distasteful.

Among nearly forty workfellows there was but one with whom I could hold any intercourse beyond that of mere civility, or the neighbourly regard which one man owes to another on the ground of their common nature. For this one, however, I speedily felt a more than ordinary esteem; an esteem which, ere long, ripened into a hearty friendship, which, in defiance of all adverse influences or circumstances, still continues.

The tenure by which journeymen tailors hold their employment is more than ordinarily slight. No workman of this craft can be sure of remaining in his present master's service after he has finished the garment he has in hand; consequently there are many and frequent changes of workfellows to him who happens to retain his station, as I did, for several years. During these years I saw many such changes, and became thereby acquainted with many different men, some of whom deserve a passing notice: here, however, I must so far restrain myself, as to bring only one before the reader. He was a good-looking man, whose dress and manners bespoke him to be superior to the generality of working tailors. From several circumstances I judged him to be a broken master, who had found it needful to retire from London to the comparative seclusion of a country-town. I soon discovered that he was a very superior workman; and also, that he possessed a large amount of business knowledge, not only in his own trade, but also in others. He was moreover well informed upon many other subjects besides those of mere business; and, being both a ready and an intelligible speaker, was able to communicate what he knew in a very clear and satisfactory way. I am indebted to him for some very judicious and sober advice—by following which I have often had the pleasure of seeing that the comfort of those around me has been promoted. He was also a thoroughly good-tempered man, and willing to do a good turn for any of his workfellows. I wish he had been *all of a piece*, but, unhappily for himself, he was not, as he could descend quite as low as any around him, both in language and demeanour: this grieved and also perplexed me; for I could not comprehend how it was that a man who must have felt his mental superiority over those around him, could voluntarily descend to their disreputable language and habits.

In resuming my personal story I must record another of my ill-advised actions. At the General Parliamentary election in 1812, the representation of my native town was sought by three candidates, the number to be returned being but two. In the contest that followed I was employed as an overseer at one of the public-houses where the non-resident voters were lodged and fed during their stay in the town. My duties were to see that these persons were duly provided for; and, further, to prevent the resident free-burgesses from having any entertainment at the candidate's expense, lest he should, if elected, be in danger of losing his seat by the operation of the Act of Parliament commonly called 'The Treating Act.' Had I reflected a moment I should have seen that I was wholly unfit for an office like this; and, therefore, ought not to accept it. I might have done this with a good grace, because I had applied for employment of a very different kind, viz. that of Clerk upon the Hustings, having heard much talk about the liberal wages usually paid to the Poll-clerks; but these places were all filled before I could get a hearing; so I was induced to become the superintendent of an unreasonable, capricious throng of men, women, and children, which required a much braver spirit and stronger arm than mine to keep it in any decent order.

After the election was over I had to wait a considerable time for my wages, which, when paid, turned out to be a very paltry sum—not so much, indeed, as I could have earned at my proper occupation. When I came to review my conduct in this affair, I saw that I had acted both foolishly and culpably. I had voluntarily gone into a scene of disorder and intemperance; where people claiming to be thought civilized and reputable allowed themselves to revel in wasteful and demoralizing gratifications, such as would have reflected dishonour upon a horde of savages. I dare say the reader will believe that I have never accepted a similar office. At the request of some friends I soon after this time became a Sunday-teacher in a school, which, during the other days of the week, was conducted upon the plan of the once celebrated Joseph Lancaster. Here my object could not be pecuniary gain, for the work was gratuitously done, and I was, moreover, put to a small weekly expense in the way of subscribing to a fund, which the Associated Teachers had established for the purpose of giving the sick or otherwise needy children some substantial relief, in addition to their religious instructions.

I must now advert to my health, which at this time gave tokens of being much impaired: the symptoms were such as usually accompany a much disordered state of the digestive powers. My diet, occupation, and amusements were alike unfavourable to my restoration; while the medicines I took for the purpose of strengthening the stomach increased the constipation of the intestinal organs, and thus did quite as much harm in that direction as they did good in the other. The evil, which I judge to have been constitutional, was, I think, much aggravated by frequently suffering the stomach to go too long without nourishment, especially in the early part of the day. My work required my attention at, or before, 5 o'clock in the morning; and, as I dared not drink water, much less beer, or any other heavy or exciting liquor at that early hour, and yet had no appetite for solid food, unless I had something to drink with it

I had no alternative but to brave the morning air—often raw and cold—with an empty stomach, and then work until 8 or 9 o'clock before I took my breakfast. It commonly occurred that, by this time, my stomach was unable to digest what it otherwise so much needed; as a natural consequence, it frequently refused to retain the food which I then took, except at the expense of more pain than was consistent with my continuing at work; I was therefore obliged to relieve it, and then I had to work for nearly five hours longer before I took any further nourishment. I was ignorant of the probable issue of my ailments, or, perhaps, I should have been less tranquil than I usually was; yet, as mental anxiety would but have aggravated the mischief, it was, I think, well for me that I could not foresee the severe and incurable disorder that was to come upon me in future years. Perhaps a part of my subsequent suffering might have been avoided had I been better acquainted with what was suitable, or otherwise, in the way of diet and warmth. I now see that I erred very much in both of these particulars, and, for the sake of a reader who may either be a fellow-sufferer, or likely to become so, I will just state wherein I was wrong. In regard to diet, I did wrong in continuing to take solid and heavy food after I found that it seldom failed to produce uneasy sensations in the stomach, head, &c. I have since learned by experiment that I further erred in using milk and sugar with the tea or coffee that I drank; and further, that I ought to have taken greater care to relieve the feet from that death-like coldness to which they have always been subject, even in the hottest weather. I have good reason to believe that I should have received much relief from a cup of *plain* and *strong* coffee, with a piece of bread or biscuit as soon as possible after I arose in the morning—at any rate before I went out into the cold air. I did not, however, until many years afterwards, learn the efficacy of coffee prepared in this way, or I should not have gone without it. My kind-hearted and ever-watchful mother would have taken care to provide either this or any other refreshment or nutriment that was within our reach. She knew of my disordered state, but was, of course, ignorant of its probable consequences, and also of the necessity there was that I should take such diet only as might be easily digested. All her kind efforts, therefore, were directed towards providing for me such as she judged to be both palatable and nutritious. She had her own way entirely, in all that pertained to my food, lodging, and other personal matters; for I never gave her any directions, having, as I judged, better employment than that of superintending the affairs of a thoughtful housewife. By the way, I will just state that I have followed the same rule ever since I have been a married man. I have always thought it to be far more within my proper sphere of action to aim at providing what might buy food, or other necessaries, than to be giving orders about either dinners or any other meals. As a natural consequence, I have ever found, from both mother and wife, an unwearied attention to my personal comfort. I have never found fault, or even seemed to be dissatisfied, with anything which I had reason to believe was done with a view to my comfort; and thus my faithful and affectionate helpers have never been discouraged in their endeavours to promote my well-being. In all this I not only followed the bent of my own temper, but also acted upon the advice of the shrewd, observant shopmate of whom I have already given a brief account.

My narrative has now come down to the winter of 1812-13, at the end of which I was called upon to act as a day's-man between the master-tailors of the town and my fellow-workmen in a negotiation relative to an advance of wages. This advance was rendered needful by the increasingly high prices of all the necessaries of life, together with the extra work required by the changes of fashion in making up clothes since the current rate of wages was fixed. I here saw a striking instance of the good effects resulting from acting respectfully towards the masters in the transaction of business of this kind. Our demands were moderate, and were made in the shape of a request, giving our reasons for making them. They were made in writing, a copy being left with each master for his private consideration, and a time being named when his answer would be looked for. They saw by the simultaneousness of their respective workmen's movements that they were acting in concert, although in a respectful manner. They therefore soon proposed a conference, at which, after some little hesitation on the masters' side, and a good deal of trouble to keep the wrong-headed among the workmen from behaving offensively, the advance of wages was agreed upon, and was thenceforth freely paid.

H

While, however, these more familiar matters claimed the chief part of my attention, I could not let the extraordinary events which were then almost daily occurring in the great political world pass without notice. Several of my shopmates were quite as much struck as myself with these unlooked-for events, and, this being so, we had a good many conferences respecting them, in lieu of the balderdash, the ribaldry, or the worse-than-childish squabbling which usually formed the staple of the shop-board conversation.

These men, with several others whose curiosity began to be awakened by the tenor of our political gossip, united with myself in subscribing for a *weekly* newspaper. We would gladly have taken a *daily* journal, but our pockets would not allow of so costly an indulgence. The paper we took was called 'The News.' Its arrival was looked for with very considerable interest, so anxious were we to see some bulletin of the Great Napoleon respecting his military operations, with the other articles of foreign news, and the commentaries of the newspaper editor. The perusal of the paper, with the conversation ensuing thereon, made the day of its coming a " white day " in our estimation.

Occasionally a debate would ensue between the sturdy John Bullites and those who were dazzled by the exploits of the French emperor. This debate would sometimes wax rather warm; it then naturally fell into a personal squabble, and when this was over it ended, as controversies generally do, by each of the disputants being the more strongly confirmed in his previous notions. Yet these little tongue-battles, abating the foolish personalities, were not without their use, inasmuch as they served to enliven the conversation, and further to fix the attention of the mere listeners more strongly upon the matters in question.

Thus we jogged on pretty comfortably until the early part of the year 1814, when we received an accession to our numbers in the persons of about six Italians, none of whom could speak more than a few words of English, while, of course, we were altogether ignorant of

"Modern Italy's degenerate speech."

Yet, by the help of signs, and the occasional visits of one of their countrymen who acted as interpreter, we made ourselves mutually intelligible.

These brethren of the needle were the *picked* tailors among those belonging to about three thousand prisoners of war, who had been confined in the war-prisons of North Britain. They had been liberated on condition of engaging to serve against their old master. With a view to this service they were sent to the barracks of our town to be organized, clothed, and accoutred. The officers' clothing was made in our master's workshop. This large addition to our *usual* press of work in spring-time made us so busy that extra help became needful, and the services of even bad workmen were gladly accepted. Our foreign auxiliaries—although they might have been good soldiers, and certainly were very pleasant companions—were far enough from being good tailors: indeed, they seemed to regard work as a matter of small moment. Their soldier's pay was more than sufficient to supply their moderate wants, and, in consequence, they illustrated practically the homely old saying which tells us that " A pennyworth of ease is worth a penny." Yet they were not lazy men; on the contrary they kept themselves busy at their work, but without a particle of that hurry and turmoil which usually characterize English tailors when work is more than ordinarily brisk. They took great pleasure in singing, and, as we made them understand that we thought their singing to be very good, they spared neither time nor trouble to please us.

When the whole body of their comrades were ready for service we lost the company of our pleasant companions. Of course we saw them no more, yet we continued to bear them in mind with feelings of, I believe, unaffected respect. They were intended for service in the Netherlands, whose people were just then endeavouring to get rid of their French rulers; but the contest was over before the " Italian Legion" could well get to the scene of action. They were then sent to their own country, and placed at the disposal of the Sardinian monarch.

In a few weeks the war was brought to a close, and all united in celebrating its termination with much seeming satisfaction. The working people confidently looked for better times, as they still continued to think that " Peace" was invariably accompanied by " Plenty." It would have been difficult to find credence had any one asserted that a sudden change from a state of almost universal war to one of general peace could not fail to be unpropitious to a large garrison town.

CHAPTER IX.

It was about this time that my former fellow-lodger, the medical man, returned from his long campaigns in the Peninsula. He had landed at Portsmouth, and was staying there under orders to join the intended expedition against New Orleans. He remembered his old fellow-lodger, and invited him to visit Portsmouth free of all cost. His invitation was so cordial and liberal that I readily accepted it, and prepared forthwith for a journey which to me seemed a long one.

I reached London in the afternoon of the day, and immediately took a place in the Portsmouth stage-coach. When we had got a few miles on the road I found that I was in an entirely new country, but, as it was then evening-time, it soon became too dark to allow of my seeing it distinctly.

The journey took the entire night, our progress being a good deal hindered by the hills which frequently crossed the road. I had never before passed a night in travelling, and therefore was the more powerfully affected with the scenes which presented themselves, and which, being lighted up by the soft beams of the "clear, round moon," were, in my view, alternately more beautiful and more picturesque than if I had surveyed them in the full light of day. I cannot well describe the manner in which I was affected by the altered aspect of all nature. I seemed almost as if I had just awoke, and found myself in a new and original world.

As we passed through the different towns and villages which lay on our road I could have fancied that we were traversing the "cities of the dead;" yet the impression was one that had nothing about it of a dreary or melancholy character. Among the few sounds that struck my ear, that of the horn, which the guard winded as often as we neared or left the "habitations of men," was the most "strangely pleasing." Although one of the meanest and most unimpressive sounds by daylight, I felt it to be suggestive of grave thoughts, and the source of lively emotions, when heard in the silence and among the shadows of the night.

My travelling companions, especially after nightfall, were not very talkative. I therefore was the more at liberty to give full scope to my fancy, whose varied, though perhaps rather extravagant flights added not a little to the pleasure of my journey.

At length the day broke, and then the play of the imaginative faculty gave place to the dictates of sober reason. The evidence of the external senses reminded me that I was in a world of realities, and not of shadows. I began to feel drowsy, and for a time lost myself in a needful slumber. When I awoke from this I found that the sun had fairly risen, and, moreover, that we were creeping up a very steep hill, into which the road was cut deep enough to form a bank of considerable height on either side. Thus there was nothing to be seen but a long narrow trough, in which it was vain to look for any attractive features, being very bare of everything in the shape of either animal or vegetable life. Ere long, however, we reached the summit of the acclivity, and then I beheld a most glorious and magnificent prospect,

" Stretching far away
From inland regions to the distant main,"

and comprising a greater number of grand and beautiful features than I had ever before seen at one view. I cannot adequately express the wonder and delight with which I contemplated a scene in which ocean, earth, and sky seemed to vie with each other in grandeur or beauty. As a whole it was admirably adapted to awaken adoration and gratitude towards the Divine Being, and to excite a lively regard for the beautiful scenes and the social advantages of one's native land. I certainly felt this regard for mine, and was ready to apostrophize it in the language of one who was both a patriot and a poet :—

" Island of bliss! amid the subject seas
That thunder round thy rocky coasts, set up,
At once the wonder, terror, and delight
Of distant nations, whose remotest shores
Can soon be shaken by thy naval arm;
Not to be shook thyself, but all assaults
Baffling, as thy hoar cliffs the loud sea-wave."

About nine o'clock in the morning I ended my journey, and was received by my friend with a right hearty welcome. I stayed with him a full week, during which time I was much at home, and also well amused. He gave me an account of his adventures during his campaigns in Portugal and Spain, together with what befel him during his service in the south of France. His habits of observation, together with his power of well-remembering, made his narratives very pleasing, especially as they were accompanied by many descriptions of interesting scenes (both in nature and art), and also by numerous anecdotes illustrative of the condition, character, and manners of the Portuguese, Spanish, and French people. I found a good deal of amusement in looking over the engravings in a Spanish volume called, I think, 'The Visions of Don Quevedo.' It was, of course, a book from which I could get but little information in the way of reading. The plates, however, told a tolerably clear story, and my host, who had learned something of the Spanish language, gave me such explanations as were necessary to my fully comprehending the meaning of the illustrations. I was a little surprised that a book which made so free as this appeared to do with the character and conduct of great and authoritative people should, in a country like Spain, have been permitted to see the light.

I was, moreover, much interested by what I saw of Portsmouth and its immediate vicinity. The fortifications of the town, at first sight, rather disappointed me, as they seemed to be inadequate to the purposes for which such works are intended; but my friend, who had seen a good many fortified places, so far explained their nature and uses as to enable me to see something of their appropriateness and efficiency.

A short boat-excursion gave me an opportunity of

seeing a little of the Dock-yard and Arsenals. I was almost astonished at the extent of these vast establishments, together with the many and great operations which were going on; but the convict-labourers, chained together and working like beasts of burden, were a sad spectacle; as also were their quarters, the prison-ships.

On this excursion I learned something concerning the capacity for stowage in large ships. My friend had business to do on board an old 50-gun ship, then used as a receptacle for medical stores. Had I not seen it, I could hardly have been brought to believe that a vessel which, when viewed at a little distance, seemed to be of only a moderate size, could have contained so vast a mass of stores as it did; and which, large as it was, left ample room for the operations of the work-people employed, and also for the accommodation of visitors. As we returned I was enabled to form a juster notion than before of the real dimensions of a first-rate man-of-war. The 'Nelson,' a new ship of, I believe, 120 guns, had just anchored in the harbour. Our boatman brought his wherry close under the stern of this huge floating citadel. I was fairly astonished at its colossal proportions, and greatly pleased with the architectural arrangements and ornaments of the part immediately before us. Even now I cannot but wonder how so ponderous a mass as this, together with all its men, guns, ammunition, and stores, can be made available for its required purposes.

The most pleasant and attractive parts of the town are the walls, especially the sea-ward line and that which looks towards Gosport and the Harbour. These being easy of access, broad and shaded by trees, form a public walk which struck me as being much more than merely agreeable, especially in the early morning time and in the evening. At the latter season it was, while I was there, worthy of being deemed beautiful, as the sea was tranquil, and illumined by the beams of the moon. There were numerous vessels under sail, together with many row-boats, from some of which might be heard the strains of music.

My friend had a good deal to do in order to be prepared for his approaching voyage. While he was attending to these matters, I usually remained at home and read in such books as I found at hand. Among these was a copy of Mr. Hoole's translation of Tasso's 'Jerusalem Delivered,' which poem I now read for the first time, and with much interest.

At the request of our landlady, I looked over a volume of Sermons by the eminent Unitarian minister Dr. Price. I did this, however, out of mere courtesy; for, although I have no objection to read any regular treatise on theological subjects, I have never been much disposed to read sermons. I ventured to report so favourably concerning these discourses, that the good woman was quite satisfied that she would do well to read them. She was the more readily brought to this conclusion, because—at which the reader may well smile—she took me to be nothing less than a clergyman! Hereby "there hangs a tale," which I cannot persuade myself to omit telling. From my early manhood, it has been my lot to be usually regarded by strangers as belonging to the clerical order; but as I have never affected the garb nor aped the manners of a reverend and "learned clerk," I attribute the mistake to less discreditable causes. It must, I think, have arisen from my usually thoughtful aspect, together with my quiet demeanour when I get into the company of strangers. At these times I am too closely engaged in trying to discover what sort of people I am with to have either time or inclination to engage in desultory talk. I can truly affirm that I despise the ridiculous vanity which leads one to aim at seeming to be something greater or wiser than he really is. It is many years ago since I read the fable which narrates the disasters that came upon a certain long-eared quadruped through his folly in assuming the skin of the forest-king. But I have never forgotten its moral, nor in any great degree acted contrary to its tenor.

This leads me to notice that I have many times had to tell well-meaning people why I have not sought to become a teacher of religion. My answer has been that I did not see myself to be a fitting person for such an office. In this I was perfectly sincere; for although my natural love of retirement and my taste for reading might, had opportunity offered, have led me to some quiet nook by the banks of Isis or of Cam, yet I could not have easily brought myself to regard these predilections as a sufficient qualification for the sacred office.

Having staid my full time at Portsmouth, I prepared for my return home, and having enunciated the unwelcome word "farewell" to my generous and esteemed friend, I set out on my journey; while he went to complete his preparations for his coming voyage, over

———— "the wide Atlantic wave."

As my homeward journey was performed by daylight, I had a more extensive and distinct view of the country than it was possible to get when I first saw it. We stopped for breakfast at an inn about eighteen miles from Portsmouth. Our breakfast room was at the back part of the house, and was lighted by a large and deep bay-window, from which there was a widely-extended and very beautiful prospect,—a truly English landscape, such an one, probably, as suggested the following animated description:—

"Heavens! what a goodly prospect spreads around,
Of hills, and dales, and woods, and lawns, and spires,
And glittering towns, and gilded streams, till all
The stretching landscape into smoke decays!"

All my travelling companions were agreeable people, but I could not avail myself of the conversation of more than two. These were a disbanded military officer and a discharged sailor. The first was a courteous man, whose language and manners bespoke him to be a gentleman. He was not disposed to be taciturn, and therefore soon began to converse both with myself and the veteran sailor, who turned out to be a truly pleasant companion. It was at or about the commencement of the shooting season, which caused the officer to introduce the subject of the field-sports common at that time of the year. This to me was rather a perplexing topic—so much so, indeed, as to make me fearful of getting into an awkward predicament. I, however, got on pretty well, as I had learned a little about these things from books and newspapers; perhaps, also, I acquitted myself all the better by taking care not to pretend to have much knowledge respecting them; and, moreover, by contriving as often as I could to put myself in the position of a learner. Thus I avoided disgracing myself, while I gained some information respecting fowling-pieces, dogs, partridges, and the like.

Sometimes, however, the conversation took another direction, and then I was less apprehensive of falling into any very egregious blunders. Yet here also I endeavoured to be the learner, and not the teacher: a plan which I heartily commend to all untaught or inexperienced persons.

The sailor was a good specimen of the true British seaman—frank, hearty, profuse, and careless of the *future*, so long as he could make a jovial time of the *present*.

In due time I reached home, and was very well pleased with my excursion. I was, however, sorry to find that my health had not been improved thereby. Perhaps this was owing in some measure to my own imprudence. During my stay at Portsmouth, I partook rather freely of shell-fish and fruit, both of which were in my case very indigestible articles. I now paid dearly for my recent indulgence; having a sense of great weight and deadly coldness in the stomach, from which I did not recover for about a fortnight. My only excuse was that I did not fully know the impropriety of my eating either raw fruit or shell-fish of any description. From that time, however, I have been more cautious, so that I have seldom again suffered from similar causes. I have, indeed, for more than twenty years almost entirely abstained from every article of diet which I have found to be difficult of digestion, however palatable it may have been, or however much I may have had an appetite for it.

On my return home I forthwith resumed my accustomed employment and amusements. Work was still plentiful, as the breaking up of the large military establishment in the barracks was not yet completed, and therefore the trade of the town had not as yet felt much of the depression which ensued upon the total loss of that large market.

During the winter I thought little about public affairs, as they were in a quiet state, except as regarded the unhappy contest with the United States or America. In this I could not take any but a painful interest, for I could not bring myself to look upon it in any other view than that of a most unnatural and profitless quarrel. As to my fellow-workmen, they took their respective sides according to the tenor of their political opinions; some wishing all manner of success to the Americans, while others felt concerned for the honour and well-being of their countrymen. When I took part in these controversies it was with a view to reconcile the opposing parties, by showing them that there was no room for any other feelings in respect of this war than those of unmitigated regret.

But ere long both this and every other public affair was thrown into the shade by our hearing that the Emperor Napoleon had left Elba, for the purpose of re-asserting his claim to the crown of France. This portentous, and to us wholly unexpected, event supplied us with much new matter for political gossip. Meanwhile all that had been done in the way of breaking up the garrison was quickly repaired. All the previous quiet was forgotten; while the preparations for war were instantly begun, and thenceforward carried on with almost incessant activity. Skeleton regiments arrived in quick succession, for the purpose of being filled up, and otherwise prepared for foreign service. The roll of the drum, the shrill notes of the "spirit-stirring fife," with the sonorous tones of trumpets and bugles, again greeted our ears, and brought back all the warlike feelings and thoughts which, for the few preceding months, had been in a state of abeyance. There was an almost continual influx into the barracks of men, stores, ammunition, and all the other materials of war. The tradespeople of the town, together with the farmers and market-gardeners of the neighbourhood, were busy in supplying the wants of the garrison, and were all sanguine in their hopes of another long-continued time of prosperity.

Ere long, however, the decisive battle of Waterloo extinguished all their hopes of a long contest. Preparations were again made for a state of peace. In the course of a few months the garrison was dispersed, the barracks were demolished, and the people of the town and its vicinity were thrown upon their own resources. These soon turned out to be very unequal to the required purposes, and, in consequence, there was soon much depression and adversity. Many of those who during the war had been large contractors for the supply of various articles to the army, and who, therefore, were thought to be *wealthy* men, now turned out to be *very poor*. Their fine houses were abandoned, their expensive style of living was laid by, and they sank down to a comparatively humble state; in some cases, indeed, into actual poverty and want.

I could not fail to perceive that a disastrous time was coming; and, further, that it would not quickly pass over. This, together with a wish—perhaps a natural one to him who has previously lived there—again to live in the metropolis, led me to resolve upon once more changing my quarters, which I soon afterwards did, fully intending to make London my future and settled home.

CHAPTER X.

I HAD secured a lodging in London prior to leaving home. My landlord was a worthy man, whom I had known for several years. He considered me rather as an inmate than as a mere lodger, and thus I was made all the more comfortable; for I regularly took my place with him and his family. Our little circle was made additionally pleasant by the presence of my landlady's brother, who lodged in the house: he was a respectable and equally agreeable man. By trade he was a spectacle-frame maker. As I sometimes visited his workshop, I saw the processes of melting and otherwise preparing the precious metals; with those of cutting and polishing tortoiseshell and pearl. He was very ready to explain to me whatever I wished to know respecting his work: a courtesy which I took care to improve to the best of my power. As he bought his materials in their rough state, I had the better opportunity of learning the whole process through which they had to pass.

We lived in the neighbourhood of the Seven Dials —a rude, noisy, and dirty locality; yet our house was a commodious one; while the many advantages I enjoyed as a lodger were more than a counterbalance against the out-of-door disagreeables.

I again joined a tailors' "House of Call;" and, after having worked for a short time for two or three masters, was sent, as a "maker of coats," to work for a respectable master residing near Grosvenor Square, with whom I continued during the whole of the subsequent time that I resided in London. Had I remained in town I might, like some of my shopmates, have continued in his employment until this day.

My workfellows were civil men; and I made myself as much at home with them as the difference between our tastes and habits would allow. I soon acquired their good-will, which I retained by treating them with courtesy, and by doing for them such little things as were within the compass of my ability. Thus I became their news-purveyor, *i.e.* I every morning gave them an account of what I had just been reading in the yesterday's newspaper. I read this at a coffee-shop, where I took an early breakfast on my way to work. These shops were but just then becoming general. They greatly pleased me, as I could *now* get suitable and timely refreshment in the morning, and that too in a warm and otherwise comfortable room, with the very pleasant accompaniment of a *daily* newspaper. The shop I selected was near the bottom of Oxford Street. It was in the direct path by which I went to my work: I therefore lost no time by making it my breakfast-house. The landlord was a civil, cleanly man, whose unvarying attention to my comfort gained my respect. I continued to be his regular customer, until a necessary change in my road to work, caused by my removing from the Seven Dials, made it necessary to find another place of refreshment. The papers I generally preferred to read were the 'British Press,' the 'Morning Chronicle,' and the 'Statesman.' I usually contrived to *run over* the Parliamentary debates and the foreign news, together with the leading articles. By husbanding my time while dressing, walking, &c., I managed to scan the newspaper without seriously trenching upon my working hours. By much practice I eventually learned to make myself pretty well acquainted with the chief contents of a newspaper in a comparatively short time: an acquisition which I have often found to be a very useful one. My shopmates were much pleased at the extent and variety of the intelligence which I was able to give them about public affairs; and they were the more pleased because I often told them about the contents of Mr. Cobbett's 'Political Register,' as they were warm admirers of that clever and very intelligible writer. Although I did not much respect the *man*, yet I felt a good deal of interest in reading his political disquisitions, because he seemed to me to have a happy talent for making a difficult question plain to an ordinary capacity.

At home I acquired increased facilities for reading, by means of a small book-club, consisting of my landlord and a few of his friends. Of this I became a member; and thus had the means of becoming a little acquainted with works which I had not before seen. Among these was Rollin's 'Ancient History,' which greatly pleased me, although I was at a loss to account for his *seemingly* intimate knowledge of what was done or said in the private cabinets of monarchs and warriors two or three thousand years before he wrote.

I also had some good opportunities for borrowing books; and thus read that very interesting quarto volume, Mr. Park's 'Travels in Africa.' I also read Mr. Colquhoun's large treatise on the 'Police of the Metropolis,' from which I gleaned much information and amusement. For my private and sole use, seeing that my friends had no taste for poetry, I bought Mr. Pye's translation of Horace, and was well pleased with my purchase; for I found the old " Roman poet" to be a very lively and shrewd companion. I also ventured to spend a guinea in the purchase of 'Kirke White's Remains:' a large sum for one like myself to spend at one time in buying books: yet I had good reason to be satisfied; for the work was useful to me in the way of strengthening and confirming my habits of reading and observation. I felt the more at liberty to buy a book, because I incurred no expenses on account of *other* amusements.

On Sundays I had the privilege—a great one for a working single man in London—of taking my meals with the family, and also of having a commodious seat at the family hearth. For these accommodations I was charged a very moderate price; one that could barely have covered the expense of my food. For the fire nothing was charged, although it was always a good one, and I had free access to it through the whole of the day.

Thus, although it was winter-time, I felt none of its hardships; for I had a comfortable home, and was supplied with work at good wages. I endeavoured to make the best use I could of my advantages; and, I hope, with some success. My health also was better than while I lived in the country: the warmer (and to me *medicated*) air of London being adapted to relieve my constitutional ailments. I had no need to look for amusement in new places, or among new companions; yet, when an opportunity offered itself for an hour's recreation of this sort, I did not omit to improve it. Thus on one occasion I found admission to the meeting of a literary society, and heard a discourse upon the nature and operations of the " Imagination," followed by a rather lively and, as I thought, clever debate. On another occasion I found access to the meeting of a society, before which a lecture "On the Rise and Progress of Philosophy" was read by the Reverend Dr. Collyer. At this meeting there was present that *truly* illustrious prince, the late Duke of Sussex: I thus, for once, had the gratification of being in the immediate presence of royalty. For both these pleasant additions to my usual recreations I was indebted to my landlord, who had the means of procuring tickets of admission to many different meetings, literary and otherwise.

I have alluded to my change of residence. This took place at Lady-day, 1816, when my landlord went to live in Bedford-Court, Covent Garden, a place which I have always regarded as being one of the pleasantest and most convenient of its class. During the winter, and while I was lodging in the Seven Dials, I seldom strayed far out of my necessary path in going to or from the shop, except that I sometimes spent a few minutes of my dinner-hour in looking at the splendid or curious articles exhibited for sale in Bond Street, near which my master lived. But when the spring-time came, and I had changed the place of my lodging, I often went out of my proper road, for the sake of breathing some fresher air, and of gazing on some fairer prospects than I could find in the crowded streets which led directly to my home. I therefore frequently went thither by the way of Hyde-Park, Constitution-Hill, St. James's-Park, Charing-Cross, and the Strand; a rather circuitous route, but one which I found to be very pleasant. I sometimes took a short walk in Hyde-Park during my dinner-hour, and thus secured a little recreation at no cost save that of abridging my eating-time: a sacrifice I willingly made, for the sake of the pleasure it gave both to the body and the mind. I will just add that I consider this park to be a salubrious spot. I also regard it as being in many respects beautiful; but I must not stay to note down my reasons for this opinion.

I occasionally varied my evening homeward walk; and then I either went down St. James's-Street, and along Pall-Mall and Cockspur-Street, to Charing-Cross; or walked through Hyde-Park, and down the long line of Piccadilly, to Leicester-Square and St. Martin's Lane. In both routes I gained my object—an opportunity of getting a view of the book and print sellers' shops; where I seldom failed to see something which I thought worth looking at. I thus procured pleasure without expense; and, after all, got home in good time, and, moreover, in a sober state, which was more than could be said of many among my fellow-craftsmen, whose evening pastimes were, in general, both chargeable and otherwise hurtful.

In the morning I kept the direct path to my work, as I then wanted all the time I could get for the purpose of looking over the newspaper. I did this, as usual, while I took my breakfast, which meal I now procured at a coffee-shop in Bear-Street, Leicester-Square. Here I found the additional accommodation of magazines and reviews: for reading the *current* numbers of which the proprietor made an extra charge of sixpence per month. This charge I was glad to pay, for the sake of reading the Edinburgh and Monthly Reviews, together with the Edinburgh, the European, and the Monthly Magazines.

These, however, I read in the evening, while I took my supper; for I learned to drink coffee at that meal as well as at breakfast-time. In addition to the daily newspapers, I also here saw the 'Examiner,' the 'Black Dwarf,' and, I think, some other weekly journals. I have never spent leisure time more pleasantly than at this shop. It was kept by a very respectable man, whose children assisted him in waiting upon the customers. The company was always decent, and, in general, very quiet; for the landlord resolutely discouraged all undue noise, and all irregular deportment, both in his family and among his visitors. I much regretted the good man's premature decease, and the consequent breaking up of his very convenient and comfortable arrangements. The shop soon went into other hands, and has long been occupied by a baker; of whom I have sometimes bought a roll, or a biscuit, out of regard to the *place*, which to me is suggestive of many pleasant recollections.

On Sundays I was, as in all preceding years, quite

at my ease. In the morning I attended public worship in the neighbourhood of Carey-Street, Lincoln's-Inn-Fields. In the afternoon I commonly employed myself in reading, but sometimes walked a short distance. On one of these occasions I went into the banqueting-room at Whitehall Palace, then used as a chapel for soldiers. The musical part of the service was performed by a military band of musicians, and I was well pleased with the music. I was, however, much disgusted at the bare-faced cupidity of the pew-openers; while I was not able to get much of either instruction or satisfaction from a service which was sadly deficient in the necessary points of becoming earnestness and reverence on the part of the worshippers. The painted ceiling—representing heathen gods and goddesses, together with a number of martial trophies, French and American, suspended, I think, over the communion-table, gave the place an aspect very much at variance with that which reminds one of Christianity and of its pacific and benignant author. I hardly need add, that I never again joined in the worship of this warlike temple.

I usually attended public worship in the evening at the Scotch Church in Crown Court, near Covent Garden—a plain and antique-looking building, attended by a congregation of plain people. To me, however, both the place and the service were truly interesting. Here there was nothing of a merely showy or ceremonious character, much less anything that betokened irreverence or indifference. I was greatly delighted with the singing. There were some voices, clearly distinguishable from the others, which

I thought to be singularly melodious. That of the precentor was marked by a plaintiveness of tone which I felt to be productive of pensive yet not unpleasing emotion. I have spent many a happy hour in the services of this unostentatious edifice—hours which, could they, with all their attendant circumstances, be recalled, I would gladly live over again.

In my walk homewards in the evening on which the Princess Charlotte of Wales was married, I saw a little of the preparations which were then making for her wedding. Her intended consort showed himself to the assembled populace from the balcony of a window in St. James's Palace, which gave me an opportunity of seeing him. Everybody seemed to be in high spirits, and

"All went merry as a marriage-bell;"

yet in how short a time was all this gaiety and rejoicing exchanged for almost universal sorrow and gloom! In the course of a few months the inmates of palaces were solemnly reminded that

"Pale Death, with equal foot, strikes wide the door
Of royal halls, and hovels of the poor."

I also saw something of the riots consequent upon the distressed state of the working classes in the autumn of this year (1816). From what I know of working men, I feel assured that none of reputable character ever voluntarily take part in popular commotions. Such men as these are as thoroughly fond of public tranquillity and safety as are the possessors of large wealth. In times of distress they suffer quietly, and, in general, patiently, buoyed up by the hope of better times. In times of riot their only fault is that of going to look at what is going on: thus they often get both into danger and subsequent disgrace. On the day of the rioting in London I was engaged to walk to Bow; but by the time I reached Aldgate I saw and heard quite enough to make me forthwith retrace my steps.

About midsummer of 1817 my father died, after an illness of several weeks. On this I considered what was my duty. I soon concluded that it was to send some needful help to the living, rather than to take an expensive journey out of respect for the dead. I therefore remained at my work, and remitted 5*l*. sterling to my widowed mother. It was of course a very seasonable supply, and I felt glad that I had been led to send it.

When work was slack I spent my leisure time in about the same way as I have already described, in regard to similar circumstances. The principal alteration consisted in my undertaking to mend my stockings and body linen. I could not get this *properly* done, although I offered to pay an extra price. I therefore took the job into hand, and thus saved my money, while my garments were kept in a decent condition. This is a very trifling matter to put into a book, but I note it down advisedly, in the hope that it may give a useful hint to some young men now in similar circumstances.

I omitted to mention in its proper place another of my contrivances. This, however, had reference solely to amusement. In the winter of 1815-16, I resolved upon attempting to think upon a given subject when at work, and not caring to join in the shop-board conversation. I felt but small difficulty about *subjects*, but was rather at a stand in respect of the dress or shape into which I should put my thoughts. I soon decided it should be into that of rhyme, and immediately set about tagging verses. This I did until it became so much of a habit that I have engaged in it at all times, in all places, and under every variety of circumstances. Before I was properly aware of the fact, I have many times been thus occupied. I amused myself by making rhymes for about ten years, during which time I generally had something, in the shape of verse, upon which I employed my thoughts, when I could lawfully detach them from more pressing matters. I thus accumulated a rather large stock of verses, in different measures and on various subjects. Much of this has been destroyed. The remainder has been several times revised. In each of these revisions it has been greatly altered and abridged. A good many pieces have been printed in a respectable although little known Magazine. Several have appeared in other publications. I have seen them commended in print. My only *other* recompense has been the *pleasure* I felt in composing them. I have now as many unpublished pieces as would make a volume of moderate size, but I dare not think of publishing them while *real* poetry is little better than a mere drug in the literary market. Will the reader bear with me if I transcribe one piece as a specimen? If it escape his censure I must be content, for as I am not a poet I cannot claim a poet's praise :—

EVENING.

Sinks the sun in western skies;
In the east dun shadows rise:
Now the clouds are ting'd with gold;
O'er the stream blue mists are roll'd.
Now the cool refreshing breeze
Gently whispers through the trees;
Now the curfew-bell is rung,
And the old tower, ivy hung,
Far reverberates the sound
Through the vales and rising ground.
Now the shepherd to the fold
Drives his flock, first duly told;
While his faithful dog goes round,
Catching every distant sound;
Nor his charge will he forsake
Till the rosy morn shall wake.
Now the bat is on the wing;
Nightingale and sedge-bird sing:
Other birds are in their nests;
E'en the bee from labour rests.
Crickets chirp their merry strain;
Glow-worms light their lamps again.
Now the " star of eve " is seen,
Harbinger of night's fair queen.
Now the peasant homeward hies,
And, with heart-felt gladness, spies
On the margin of the green,
By a stranger seldom seen,
His secluded quiet cell,
Where 'tis his blest lot to dwell
With the partner of his life,
Free from discontent and strife:
Where he seeks and finds the bliss
Which the sons of pleasure miss.

After my father's death I met with nothing that much affected me until the occurrence of that event which seemed to touch the hearts of the entire British people. I stay not to speculate upon the causes of that universal favour with which the deceased princess was regarded. That she was the object of the nation's unaffected good wishes, and the anchor of its hopes, were facts too palpable to admit of dispute. In these feelings I warmly participated, and ventured to hope that I might partake of the benefits expected to result from her assumption of sovereign authority. I was ill prepared for the unexpected event which blighted this hope, and seemed to spread a dark cloud over all that had gilded the future. But it was not on these grounds alone that I felt regret. There were other and better feelings called into exercise. I could not help grieving at the sudden wreck of life, with all its enjoyments, on the part of one whose age, character, and pursuits seemed to promise her a more than ordinary share of happiness. The affecting circumstances of her death added greatly to the painful emotion which that event, under a milder aspect, would then have produced. I was truly much more grieved than I should previously have thought possible on account of any one but a near and tenderly beloved relative. The plaintive remonstrance of the ancient patriarch, "Wherefore hast thou made all men in vain?" forced itself upon me, in spite of the conviction that I ought rather to say, "Shall not the Judge of all the earth do right?"

On the evening of the funeral I was alone, and in a very quiet place, being engaged to keep house for a friend. I thus distinctly heard the solemn tolling of the numerous bells which announced that the mortal remains of one who was so lately among the happiest of the living were about to be consigned to the "grave's narrow house." I never had a more pressive lesson upon the precariousness of human life, or the fleeting shadowy character of earthly grandeur and felicity. I did not fully recover my usual tranquillity of feeling for several weeks, or rather months, after the occurrence of this disturbing event.

I should have liked to purchase an engraved portrait of the deceased princess, but was utterly unable to determine which of the numerous different ones on sale was a likeness. They differed so widely, even those executed by artists of reputation, that but for the lettering I certainly should not have judged them to be intended to represent the same person. I have often, in other cases, had occasion to notice a similar difference, and have been at a loss to account for it, except in a way not creditable to the respective artists. In spite of all that I have read or heard to the contrary, I still venture to think that portraits ought to be *faithful* imitations of their originals, otherwise I do not see of what use they are or can be. They cannot, at any rate, assist the spectator to form a correct opinion concerning the true aspect and probable character of the person represented.

I now come to the year 1818, in the spring-time of which I made an excursion into Hertfordshire; walking, by way of Edgeware, to Watford, and riding from thence to Hemel-Hempstead in a *returning* post-chaise. This was one of the most delightful holidays of my life. I had long been confined to London or its immediate vicinity, and therefore the transition from a scene of noise and turmoil, and mere worldliness, to one of rural quiet and beauty, was truly refreshing. It was made still more so by its suddenness. After I got beyond Edgeware I felt myself to be in the country. At Watford I staid to get refreshment, fully intending to foot it all the way to where I was going. This I was prevented doing by the weather becoming showery. I therefore ventured upon the expense of riding, and a most pleasant ride it was; for the showers and sunshine alternated, and thus the scenes around me became, as I thought, additionally beautiful, as within a short time I saw them under two different aspects. For a considerable distance the road skirted a large park. The rays of the declining sun, beaming through the foliage of its plantations, and irradiating my pathway, gave occasion to my imagination for thinking about other and yet more enchanting scenes. It was after sunset when I reached my journey's end. The evening was delightfully clear and serene; the air cool, yet soft and fragrant; while the animal creation was either silent, or gradually becoming so. The following morning was equally, although differently, beautiful. It was most resplendently bright and animating. My heart rejoiced both at the "season and the scene," for I felt both to be eminently cheering. Before I returned to London I went by a cross-road to St. Albans. In my walk I stopped to get some refreshment at a rustic alehouse, whose landlady, a very decent-looking, civil woman, seemed almost surprised at being asked for "a cup of tea." After some doubting and difficulty the necessary ingredients were hunted up, and at length I got some palatable, although not very strong, tea, with bread and butter. As to milk or cream, my hostess seemed to have no means of furnishing either the one or the other. Yet I was very well pleased with my inn; for although it was a humble one, in fact the humblest I had ever seen, still everything was clean, and in tolerably good order. I thought St. Albans to be a pleasant little town. A large ecclesiastical structure, principally in ruins, struck me as having once been very magnificent.

It was about this time that I first read that very beautiful poem, 'The Pleasures of Hope.' I also reperused a large portion of Cowper's Poems; and, in spite of the unfavourable accounts of it given by critics, resolved upon reading Thomson's 'Liberty.' This resolution I carried into effect, to my very considerable amusement, if not instruction. As to its poetical merits, I did not venture to sit in judgment upon them.

I now found out another pleasant spot for an evening walk, which, moreover, was at a very convenient distance from my lodging. This was none other than Waterloo Bridge, over which there was so little traffic of any sort as to leave the bridge in a most quiet, inviting state for a saunterer like myself. I thought the penny charged for toll a very cheap price for the privilege of walking at my ease, and breathing the fresh air as long as I pleased; yet I think it would have given me more satisfaction to have seen such an amount of traffic over this magnificent structure as would have given the shareholders in the concern a fair return of interest upon their enormous outlay of capital.

The calling of a new Parliament gave me an opportunity of seeing the way in which a Westminster election was sometimes conducted. I have seldom witnessed a more disorderly scene than that which was exhibited at and near the hustings during the long period of fourteen or fifteen days. The contest was prolonged until the latest hour allowed by law, through the folly of one candidate, the then celebrated Mr. Henry Hunt, who polled, after all, no more than about eighty votes. His partisans were men of the lowest character, whose unruly and frequently riotous conduct greatly impeded the business of the election. They did much damage to several houses occupied by the committees or friends of the candidates to whom they were hostile. Their rioting was several times of so serious a character as to call for the interference of a military force. This they insulted in the grossest manner, although, whenever it was directed by the magistrate to disperse them, they fled with the greatest precipitation into the market-place, and sheltered themselves in its nooks and corners, where the soldiers could not follow them without risking the safety of their horses. Some of the stragglers, however, got smart blows from the broad-sides of the soldiers' swords, at which I was glad, and only wished that each delinquent could have been punished in like manner, for I was indignant at their ruffianly conduct. What I here saw of mob law, together with what I had previously seen of it on several other occasions, inspired me with a real horror at the thought of mob government, and led me to conclude that by far the worst despotism is that which such a government exercises.

The only gratifying circumstance in this long and

wearisome election was the manner in which that great and good man, Sir Samuel Romilly, was elected. There was no noise or show on either his part or that of his friends, yet he was returned at the head of the poll, and numbered among his supporters a very large portion of the truly respectable men of Westminster. I felt deeply grieved at his premature death; and the more so, because of the lamentable circumstances that led to it. This event was, I think, regretted by men of all political parties. The great heat of the summer gave me much bodily inconvenience—so much, indeed, at times as made me consent to sacrifice an afternoon's earnings, for the sake of getting into a cooler place than a tailor's workshop. On these occasions I usually went into the shaded parts of Hyde-Park or of Kensington Gardens. In the latter I remember to have passed one afternoon in a very pleasant way. I sat in a quiet, well-shaded spot, where I had the benefit of a cool atmosphere, and read once more Dr. Beattie's ' Minstrel '—a poem which pleases me *now* quite as much as it did *then*. It is one of the poems of which I am never weary; from which circumstance alone, were there no other evidence, I should be led to infer that it is true poetry—the poetry of the heart no less than of the imagination. Some of my shopmates, who were oppressed in like manner as I was, went, for the professed purpose of being more cool, to drink porter and to play at skittles or Dutch-pins—for which folly I rallied them pretty freely, and I hope with some good effect.

There was much curious speculation among scientific men as to the causes and probable consequences of the unusual heat of the season. I read some of these, and was thereby half-persuaded that Great Britain and other northern countries were about to enjoy the advantages of the tropical regions. I hardly need say that all these pleasing visions were ere long effectually dissipated by a return to our usual temperature, or rather, to one more than usually cold and variable. I have ever since had less faith in theories hastily constructed upon a few accidental or isolated facts.

CHAPTER XI.

HITHERTO I have not directly touched upon *that* subject which, above all others, may be said to be of universal interest, and which, therefore, has so prominent a place in almost all books that treat of human feelings and actual experience. Herein I have acted advisedly; I did not think it either needful or prudent to narrate my own thoughts and feelings upon this subject. They will be easily conjectured by such as know the power of a lively and creative imagination; while such as do not, would be unable rightly to understand what might be stated concerning them. It will hardly have been supposed by any one that I should have lived for nearly twenty-seven years without frequently thinking upon a matter which " comes home to men's bosoms "—if not to their " business "—in a way so forcible as this generally does. In good truth, I had thought about it both frequently and anxiously long before I was twenty years old. Indeed, were I disposed to be *fully* explicit upon this matter, I could tell more than one little tale, referable to my very early life, at which some would perhaps smile; while others might be a little sceptical. The feelings were childish enough, in all conscience, as were the incidents that produced them. Yet, childish as they were, I have never been able to account for them in a satisfactory way. After my seventeenth year, my feelings were not difficult to interpret, although for several years they were perhaps more than sufficiently romantic and changeable. Yet, had they been less so, I had not so long remained a bachelor. I could not procure the means of accommodating what I saw to be the *realities* of a working-man's domestic life to the desires of the heart; and thus I allowed year after year to glide away, until the visionary feelings that made me hesitate, had given place to those of a more sober and matter-of-fact character. By the aid of these I felt content to take things as I found them, and to give up my long-cherished wishes for what I now saw was wholly unattainable. This change was, doubtless, partly brought about by the mere lapse of time; but it was also, in part, the result of much observation, and some reading. As to the latter, I could not find much that suited my purpose. I read a volume which was called 'The Guide to Domestic Happiness,' but found that it had no direct bearing upon the case of a working-man—all its reasonings, counsels, and encouragements being based upon the supposition of the reader's being a person of substance and education. The only publication I met with which at all came up to my wishes was one called 'Letters on the Marriage State;' but even this bore only in a distant way upon the case in question. What I wanted was a book which would give me some additional information as to the best means of duly attending to business, without that total neglect of mental culture so common among working people and little tradesmen. After all, however, I was left pretty much in the same state as before I had consulted these guides. Still I was disposed to believe that I might find enough leisure time for engaging a little in intellectual pursuits and pleasures without any neglect of positive duties. I therefore resolved, when opportunity offered, to make the experiment, and it was not long ere I saw a prospect of being able to do so. This brings me to observe that towards the close of 1818 I casually met with my future wife. We had known each other for nearly ten years, and, moreover, were well acquainted with each other's previous history. We had seldom met, and then, as in the present instance, quite accidentally. On this occasion, however, it occurred to me that we might very properly see each other more frequently. I thought thus, because I *now* seriously intended to make her my future companion, provided she were content and at liberty to be so; for, while I hesitated about becoming a married man, I would not allow myself to keep company with a woman, lest I should do her wrong either by exciting expectations that might be disappointed, or by indirectly preventing her being noticed by another man. I had learned to believe that my domestic happiness did not depend upon my having what is quaintly called a " bookish woman" for my wife, but that it would be greatly dependent upon my choosing one of plain good sense and of thoroughly domestic habits. I had now met with such an one, and, as we were not strangers, it required no hesitation on either side before deciding upon our plans for the future. Our first intention was to have remained in London; but we were subsequently led to determine upon settling in my native town. The chief reasons for this determination were —a desire to be so near to my mother as to be able to help her better than we could if living at a distance, and a hope that I might be able to establish myself in a small tailoring business on my own account. I also thought that, in the event of our having children, we should be better able to take due care of both their health and morals in a country town than we could reasonably expect to be in *such* a London residence as we should be obliged to have.

About the end of May, 1819, we were married, at St. Paul's, Covent Garden, which was my parish-church. We spent a part of our wedding-day in looking at the Royal Artists' exhibition of paintings at Somerset House, in which we found much that gave us very pleasant entertainment. Afterwards, as the day was beautifully clear and serene, we indulged ourselves with a short excursion, in a westerly direction, upon the broad and gently-flowing Thames. Within two or three days after our marriage we went into the country, and immediately set about trying to effect our purposes. Herein we found considerable difficulty, part of which was, for some time, insurmountable. Had we been able to afford it, we should forthwith have returned to London; as it was, however, we determined to do the best we could, and to wait for more favourable times. Although I could not get many clothes to make on my own account, yet I did not want for work as a journeyman. I had obtained the promise of employment at my former master's before I left London, and therefore was so far provided for. My good wife assisted me at the needle both cheerfully and efficiently. The first year of our course was a rather rough one; still we had many comforts, and some amusement. For myself, I was amply provided with the means of passing all my little leisure in a pleasant way. By the courtesy of a friend I had the loan of Mr. Pope's poetical works, together with his translations of Homer's 'Iliad' and 'Odyssey.' I also read Mr. Hervey's 'Theron and Aspasia,' but with no great pleasure, because of its chiefly dwelling upon controverted points of theology. I was induced to read it by a sense of what was due to the request of a valued friend. As to Mr. Pope's works and translations I read them with much satisfaction. In passing, I must observe that of Homer's poems I greatly preferred the 'Odyssey;' for the 'Iliad' was too full of warlike descriptions for one of my pacific temper. I still retain this preference. My reading-times were at my meals, and after I had left work in the evening. The winter was a severe one—quite enough so, indeed, to demolish all the fine theories respecting the felicitous issue of the great heat of 1818. When it was over, I began to steal a few moments occasionally for the purpose of looking upon the fair and sweet face of nature. It was at this time, I think, that I read Mr. Rogers's very beautiful poem called 'Human Life,' and also a history of the recent wars. In the early part of April my wife brought me a son—a circumstance which awakened *new* feelings, and also stirred me up to be, if possible, yet more diligent and provident in regard to household wants. Towards the close of the year

I was unable to work for a fortnight, through lameness, but we had the resource of a benefit-club, the allowance from which helped us through this difficulty pretty well. While laid by from work, I read Mr. Mackenzie's 'Man of Feeling' and other tales. I thought them a little too highly coloured to be of any great use, considered as pictures of men and manners. In the course of the ensuing spring (1821), I read Mr. Washington Irving's 'Sketch-Book.' I thought it very beautiful, and only wished that he had more fully carried his fine imaginative powers beyond

"this visible diurnal sphere."

By the way, I must observe that a similar defect exists in Akenside's 'Pleasures of the Imagination;' a poem which in every other respect gives me very great satisfaction. I also read some volumes of the 'London Magazine,' which I thought to be a very cleverly conducted publication. On the anniversary of my birth-day (July 5) my wife made me a birthday present, in the shape of a (second) son. I had not learned to consider such events as calamities, and therefore, when a well-meaning man expressed his regret at my being so heavily burthened, I frankly told him that I could not join therein, and so our conference ended.

In the autumn season I ventured to accept the invitation of a friend, who had visited me, to accompany him on his return home. We walked nearly twenty-five miles of the way thither, and thus made the journey both a *cheap* and pleasant one. On this visit I saw and went much about the extensive ruins of that once magnificent castle where the too-celebrated Queen Mary found an asylum prior to her becoming the sovereign of England. On my return, we hired a small tenement adjoining the one occupied by my mother, for our increased numbers made a change needful. We had but little room to spare, yet as a worthy and aged woman expressed a strong wish to be our inmate, we contrived to accommodate her, and had no reason to regret having done so. She was a most kind-hearted woman, and very attentive to our children. Thus she acquired and preserved our cordial esteem. She continued with us until her decease — a period of about eighteen months. I ought to have observed before now, that in the springtime of this year (1821) I began to be well supplied with work on my own account. I thought it remarkable that while I continued to seek master-work I could not succeed; whereas, when I had long given up all thought or hope about it, work came to me spontaneously, and from quarters whence I should least have looked for it. I did not feel at liberty to regard *this* as a matter of mere chance. Ere long I had so much of this kind of employment that I could not serve a master. I therefore intimated this to mine, and thus we parted company upon good terms.

The majority of my customers found their own cloth and the other principal materials, which, as I had no *capital*, was a great convenience. When I was required to supply these things I found a friend in the person of my former *juvenile* master. He had now succeeded to his late father's business, and was quite as willing to give me credit for what I wanted, in the way of trade, as he had formerly been to lend me his books. I owe him a very large amount of gratitude for very much kindness during more than *ten* years' dealings with him as a draper. He also again freely supplied me with the loan of books. At this time he lent me several volumes of the 'New Monthly Magazine,' among the many very interesting articles in which I was especially pleased with the 'Letters from Algiers,' written by Mr. Thomas Campbell, the eminent poet. Thus I found myself in as comfortable circumstances as I could reasonably have expected. My increased expenses were met by an increased income, and I felt satisfied with my condition. It was needful that I should work very closely, and for many hours on every working-day; but this was no hardship: on the contrary, I was glad to be fully employed, for the sake of being able to maintain my household.

I am now brought to the year 1822, during which I worked very hard, but still found a little time for amusement; this, of course, was at the usual seasons. During this year I read an odd volume of that *curious* publication the 'Anti-Jacobin Review,' from which I gathered a little that pleased me. Among other things I met with some views respecting the conduct of Judas Iscariot towards his Divine Master which to me were quite new. I, however, thought them both reasonable and probable. I also read Mr. O'Meara's 'Voice from St. Helena,' Dr. Henderson's 'Travels in Iceland,' and Captain Parry's 'Narrative' of his Arctic voyage. I must here beg the reader to remember that henceforth when I say that I have read any book, it will only mean that I gave it a hasty perusal, for I had no time for close reading.

In the month of December of this year I had a daughter born, to whom my aged lodger was remarkably attentive. At the close of this year, therefore, I stood in a position widely differing from that which I occupied at the close of 1818. In not more than four years I found myself transformed from a single man, almost wholly free from care, into a householder, a landlord, a husband, a father, and a little tradesman. I felt the weight of the responsibility resting upon me, yet I hoped for strength equal to the day.

The year 1823 passed on with an even course. My daily task and my household affairs underwent no change that requires any particular notice. My little business continued to increase, and I made every possible exertion to get through it without employing help. I often worked until midnight, and sometimes until a much later hour. I had but little exercise except that which I took when obliged to go out upon business. The bad effects of this unremitting application were ere long manifest. I suffered much from indigestion, and the other ailments connected therewith. Once more my asthmatic disorder began to give me some trouble. Altogether I was a good deal shattered, and had some smart fits of illness. These, however, for a time gave way to the power of medicine, and thus I was enabled to keep at my business, although with less effect than formerly. I had now frequently to employ a journeyman, not, however, so much on account of my broken health as on account of my little business continuing to increase. In addition to the help of a man, I had that of a youth who offered himself as an apprentice. He was a very industrious, clever, attentive lad, and soon made an excellent workman. He had a general notion of the business before he came into my service, having been what is called a "trotter" in a large and respectable tailoring-trade. I have great reason to respect him, and I have some grounds for believing that he respects his former master.

In the autumn of this year I left home for a week, with a view to the benefit of my health; but, as I could not afford to do this without at the same time doing some business, I tried to get orders for clothes among the friends I visited. They very cordially seconded my views, and I returned home in somewhat better health, and with orders for about five suits of clothes. During my excursion I visited London, Grays, and Gravesend, at each of which places I did some business, and moreover was kindly treated.

I made a similar journey, and with like results, in each of several following years. It must have been during this year that I began to read a work which gave me much and unalloyed pleasure: this was 'The Modern Traveller,' edited by Mr. Conder. I read the parts consecutively, and was so much pleased with them that I looked for their publication with great interest. By favour of my friendly draper I also had the high satisfaction of looking over the elegantly written and very entertaining 'Letters' of Mr. Gray, together with M. Sismondi's 'History of the Literature of the South of Europe.'

In June, 1824, my good wife gave me a *third* son. During the time of her confinement my health gave way rather seriously. Soon after she got about again I was seized by a severe illness, from which I did not recover for nearly a month. By this attack I was so much enfeebled that I was barely able, in the first stage of my convalescence, to sustain the weight of my newly-born child. From this time my health became more infirm than formerly, being frequently, and sometimes seriously, interrupted. Yet I continued to go on with no greater relaxation of my exertions than was quite imperative. I found that medicine was of but little use, and was directed to pay a strict regard to my diet, and also to the proper times for repose. I did this, and ere long found myself much relieved; but still I did not recover my former strength.

I now had much additional proof of the value of a thoughtful and affectionate domestic partner. I must not, however, enlarge upon this topic. Suffice it to say that I found mine to be unwearied in her efforts to promote my comfort by every possible means.

CHAPTER XII.

In the course of this summer I was unanimously elected a member of a literary society which numbered among its members many of the most respectable gentlemen, professional and private, of the town and its neighbourhood. It also included a goodly number of the principal tradesmen. I believe that I was the only *poor* man of the whole number. This very gratifying mark of good-will from men so much my superiors in all respects I owed to the good offices of my old and tried friend, the woollen-draper. He told me that he wished I would take courage, and allow him to propose me as a candidate. To this I consented, and through his favourable representations I was elected. I now had the privilege of hearing a good lecture monthly upon some subject of real interest, and was, moreover, kindly noticed by several gentlemen to whom I was previously a stranger. It was imperative upon *each* member to deliver a lecture in his turn, or pay a fine. This to me was a rather formidable matter even to contemplate; but I ventured to hope for some loop-hole through which I might retreat, and thus escape the dreaded ordeal. But I was not to be thus favoured. In the spring-time of 1825 my patron, who was one of the secretaries of the society, came to my house for the purpose of telling me that I was expected to take my proper turn in lecturing. I would fain have got excused by paying the appointed fine, but found that this would not be satisfactory. I therefore consented to be duly announced as a lecturer. As I was at a loss for a subject, my friend gave me one; but I felt afraid to grapple with it, and the more so because I had never read anything directly treating upon it. In fact, I was wholly ignorant of its theory. I, however, now began to get what help I could, and gave the subject all the attention I was able to give. In due time I read my lecture, and, to my great surprise, no less than to my high gratification, found that I had acquitted myself to the satisfaction of the society. The issue was, that many of the members noticed me in a very kind and encouraging way. I had the offer of the loan of any books I might want to aid me in the preparation of my *second* lecture upon the same subject, for I proposed to give a connected series; and, moreover, was favoured with the countenance of several most kind-hearted gentlemen, to whom, subsequently, I owed much gratitude for help given me in days of trouble and sickness. I *now* began to reap a recompense for the trouble I might have taken in getting a little intellectual knowledge.

I am now come to the latter part of the year 1825, at which time it seemed needful that I should procure a larger habitation—our numbers having increased to six, with the prospect of a further increase in the early part of the ensuing year. In the course of the winter I read some of Mr. Dugald Stewart's 'Essays on the Human Mind,' together with a part of Dr. Reid's on the same subject. I also read Mr. Cary's translation of Dante, and Mr. Jowett's 'Christian Researches.'

On January the 1st, 1826, I had a new-year's gift in the person of a *fourth* son. He was born very lame in one foot, but, by careful management, was thoroughly cured by the time he was old enough to require the use of it. At Lady-day I went into a larger house, and again had a lodger,—an aged and infirm military officer, who remained with us until his decease, a period of about nine months. The fatigue and anxiety I underwent in directing his funeral, and in settling his affairs, brought on a very severe illness—so severe that for some days my recovery was a very doubtful matter. Again I experienced the benefit of having a vigilant and willing nurse, one who was so attentive to the wants of her charge as to be regardless of her own. My recovery was slow, and it was a good while before I could bear the fatigue of even moderate exertion. While in this state I read the 'Letters' of Lady Mary Wortley Montagu, and some of Dr. Beattie's and Mr. Hume's 'Essays;' together with part of Dr. Beattie's 'Essay on Truth.' As the spring came on I got strength, and was far more active and useful than I could previously have hoped to be.

In March, 1827, my wife presented me with a *fifth* son, so that we had now six children, none of whom was capable of self-management. I now had three apprentices and a journeyman. Our house, therefore, was a busy scene, and the more so because our circumstances required that we should add to our income by continuing to let lodgings. Amidst all the complicated and numerous duties that now devolved upon me, I was required to prepare for reading a *second* lecture before the literary society to which I belonged. In the latter part of the spring-time I read this lecture, and *again* was successful in obtaining the approbation of my auditors. This, however, was the *last* time of my being their lecturer, as the numberless duties and cares of my station, coupled with my again declining health, effectually prevented my having time for suitable preparation. My labour, however, had not been lost. I had thereby obtained the good-will of those whose circumstances and disposition made them both able and willing to afford me substantial help at a future day.

But, though I was compelled to give up my connexion with the literary society, I did not renounce my habits of reading. My leisure-time was now truly of small amount, yet, as I took care to avoid wasting any part of it, I made it available to an extent which enabled me to read as much as, perhaps, was desirable.

At the Michaelmas sessions of our Borough Court I was called to serve on the petit jury. My brother jurymen chose for our foreman a fine-looking, portly man. From what followed I could not but think that their choice was made upon much the same principle that has sometimes governed nations in their selection of a monarch. In the course of the proceedings a prisoner was arraigned on a charge of "stealing from the person." The counsel for the prosecution soon got through his part of the case; while the prisoner's advocate seemed, as I thought, not over-zealous on behalf of his client. It seemed to be admitted that the prisoner was guilty; so that the verdict of the jury was anticipated. For myself I was not satisfied with what had been done, and therefore took courage to exercise the power belonging to a juryman, and proceeded to cross-examine both the prosecutor and his witnesses. I had some fear of being defeated in my object by reason of all the latter being allowed to be in court at the same time; yet I determined to go on, and the event proved that I was right in doing so. At first I had some difficulty, because the examinant demurred to my right of questioning him. I set this matter at rest by an appeal to the court. Ere long I succeeded in making the prosecutor, who had just deposed to some minute circumstances, admit that he had, within the space of a few hours before the robbery, drunk so much of ardent spirit as to have become nearly insensible. As to his witnesses, they did not agree in their testimony. On these grounds I doubted their evidence, and refused to agree in convicting the prisoner. I was the more unwilling to find him guilty because of the singularly good character he received from respectable people. At first I had but two of my fellow-jurors willing to go with me, but I kept to my determination, and, after the lapse of about two hours, was able to direct our foreman to say " not guilty." When the business of the day was over, I learned, to my great surprise, that when juries convicted a prisoner, it was customary for the prosecutor to give them " something to drink." Our foreman asked for this allowance, whereupon the town clerk, in a very emphatical manner, replied, "No; you say 'not guilty.'" But for the immediate breaking up of the court I should have asked whether it were lawful or becoming in a jury to look for a reward from prosecutors. I could not speak to its lawfulness, but as to its propriety I had no doubt, and therefore was heartily disgusted at it.

One of the witnesses for the prosecution was the summoning officer. He was so much offended at my having cross-examined him, that he never again gave me a summons. Thus I got rid of a duty which was too much for my strength, especially as I could not allow myself to be a merely nominal juryman.

I now come to the year 1828, at the beginning of which I was affected by a disorder of the head. For this I was let blood, by cupping in the neck; but the remedy proved worse than the disorder, for I was forthwith so feeble as to be hardly able to keep about. I did not recover from the effects of this injudicious operation for a full year. About the middle of May my wife gave me a *second* daughter. At this time I could not but be painfully solicitous about the future lot of my faithful partner and our large family of young children. My health was in so broken a state as to warrant my fears that it would not be again restored; yet I endeavoured to believe that all might yet be well with us. Meanwhile I attended to my duties as well as I could, and my ever-watchful nurse took all possible care of my health. At Michaelmas we again removed in order to accommodate a lady who wished for a lodging in the house to which we went. As she promised to be a permanent inmate, and moreover to pay a fair amount of the rent, we felt warranted in making the change. The house was commodious, and in a very pleasant situation. It also promised to be more conducive to my health than that which we previously occupied. This promise was fulfilled, for I became better soon after we had made the change. I had, however, much difficulty of various kinds to struggle with; much of which had been created by my inability to work so efficiently as I formerly could. Yet I did not give way to despondency, as I continued to have a good deal of business, and stood at a small expense for house-rent.

About this time my second son was attacked by an obstinate disorder, which baffled the efforts of medical skill. This added another to our many causes of anxiety. In the month of November our infant daughter was removed by death after a short illness. I will not attempt to describe how this event affected both myself and my wife; I will only say for myself that the deceased infant, had she lived, would, perhaps, have engrossed too large a share of my affections.

In the month of February, 1829, our *fourth* son sickened, and soon died. This new bereavement, occurring so soon after the former one, touched our hearts deeply, and the more so because of the very precarious state of our second son. Yet when we committed the inanimate body to the grave, we did it under the cheering influence of a " sure and certain hope" with respect to the departed child, combined with the belief that we should one day see him again.

But I forbear to enlarge, although the subject be one that might perhaps excuse some prolixity.

The remaining part of the year passed without the occurrence of anything very remarkable. Of course there was no lack of new incidents in a household so large as ours. We were fully occupied, and, I believe, used our best exertions to turn our labour to a useful account. As to reading, I had neither time nor strength for more than a very little, yet I did something; as I looked through a translation of the works of that eminent divine, James Arminius, with which I was well satisfied, but especially so with the prefixed memoir of his life. I had also, for a few days, the loan of Mr. Montgomery's 'Lectures on Poetry,' a book which I should have been glad to read thoroughly.

In the spring-time of 1830 I had a *sixth* son born. My wife had now brought me eight children. From this time she brought me no more. It was in this year that a heavy calamity, which had long been impending, overwhelmed my friend and creditor—the woollen-draper. From the time of his beginning business this event seemed almost inevitable, on account of the unfavourable circumstances necessarily attending it. Yet even in his misfortunes he did not forget to do me all possible service. By his representations I was enabled to make an easy settlement with the assignees of his estate, and thus was greatly relieved. I take pleasure in recording my gratitude for his truly kind and generous conduct towards me, and much regret that I have never been able to make him any return, save that of thanks.

The loss of so forbearing a creditor as he had always been, gave me much subsequent trouble. It was also the occasion of my losing several of my customers, who had been accustomed to take a rather long credit, but whom I was now forced to press for earlier payment. At this they took umbrage, and withdrew their support.

We continued to make every effort we could to get a living and to act with integrity. With these views, we crowded ourselves and children into a corner of the house, that we might have room for a *third* lodger. He proved to be a respectable, worthy man, of studious habits and pleasant manners. He had long been a commercial agent, first in South America, and afterwards at Hamburgh. He staid with us the full time which he had originally proposed to spend in our neighbourhood. During this time he gained our cordial esteem, and subsequently, by his generous conduct, acquired a right to our warmest gratitude. My other lodgers were a married couple. The husband was a Wesleyan minister. Of him I had the loan of a work which I had indeed previously read; but of which I was not tired, nor I believe ever should be. This was the "Journal" of that great and good man, the Rev. J. Wesley. I have long regarded it as being equal in interest to Mr. Boswell's 'Life of Dr. Johnson,' although its contents are, of course, very dissimilar. I also read many of his other works in the course of the *two* years during which our lodgers remained with us. I may just observe that Mr. Wesley's style of writing is eminently concise and clear; well adapted to the capacity of the uneducated reader. A Cambridge scholar has told me that he thought it remarkable also for its purity and simple elegance.

I continued to give such help as I could in a work to which my assistance was requested in the year 1829: it involved no neglect of my proper business, inasmuch as it was done only on Sundays; while it contributed to the benefit of my health, by giving me some opportunities for exercise in the open air of the adjacent country. These excursions were made in different directions, and thus had the additional charm of variety. How far they were useful to others I know not; to me, however, they were very refreshing; as in addition to their favourable bearing upon my health, they brought me into contact with many kind-hearted people, whose friendship I thus acquired: some of them had afterwards a strong claim upon our grateful esteem. I now pass on to the year 1831, during which nothing occurred that calls for particular notice, except the decease of my worthy mother. She died in the month of November, "in a good old age." The meridian of her life was overcast by dark clouds, and agitated by rude storms, but its evening-time was tolerably bright and serene; while its end was "peace." As I looked upon the composed features of a face which I had often seen expressing sorrow, or deep anxiety, I could not but rejoice that she had at length done with the cares of this troublous life, and had entered upon a state of secure and perfect rest. While subsequently thinking about her, my thoughts threw themselves into the shape of verse. Perhaps I may be forgiven if I insert the last stanza of what I then composed.

> "Mother, farewell!—whatever be the lot
>   Of us, thy children, in this world of care,
> 'Twill cheer us to reflect thou feelest not
>   One pang of all our griefs, but dwellest where
>   All is eternally secure and fair;
>   And—while we toil along our thorny way,
>   Beset with many a dread and perilous snare—
>   Hast found repose, for thou hast pass'd away
> From earth's unquiet scenes, to heaven's unruffled day."

This brings me to the year 1832, during the greater part of which our little affairs went on with a tolerably even current. I had a fair supply of work—although the greater part was such as bore only a very small profit; my health was not seriously interrupted, and we were disposed to bear up patiently under the somewhat heavy burdens which former afflictions had brought upon us. Our son, who had so long been ailing, became much better; so much so, indeed, as to encourage the hope of his being restored to good health. Thus we went on until the beginning of November, when we were called to enter upon a scene of more than ordinary labour and anxiety. Our house was already nearly crowded with inhabitants: in the daytime they numbered fifteen, and at night not fewer than eleven. An esteemed friend, who was in poor health, requested us to try to accommodate her for a short time with a lodging. She wished for a room commanding a view of the spacious and pleasant nursery-ground and market-garden which almost surrounded our dwelling. We met her wishes by giving up our bedroom. As she brought with her a nurse and a sister, our already thickly-peopled house was made inconveniently full and busy; yet we encountered the difficulty cheerfully, and struggled with it patiently. I was disordered by an asthmatic attack on the day when this new scene opened upon us, and had to resort to a rather strong dose of ipecacuanha at night in order to get relief. On the following morning I breathed with much more ease, and, although languid, set myself diligently and resolutely to work; our invalid son, as was his constant habit, did all he could to help us. He over-exerted himself, however, and, being further injured by a heavy fall, soon relapsed, and became seriously ill. Our friend also continued to get worse. This went on until the latter part of December, when our son died, and our friend followed him in about thirty-six hours afterwards—both of them being worn down and exhausted by severe and almost unintermittent suffering. Our Christmas-day was a day of sadness, yet not wholly unrelieved, for, while we were grieved at our double bereavement, we felt assured that, in each case, we might

"Congratulate the dead, and crown the tomb
With wreaths triumphant."

The face of our deceased friend was marked by an expression of acute suffering, which made it painful to look upon; her last hours of life were, indeed, hours of sharp conflict with physical disorder, but her spirit was unbroken, for she looked confidently for a better and brighter state of being. On the countenance of our departed son, whose death was unattended by pain, there was, from the moment of his departure until the close of the third day afterwards, an air of happy repose, such as I have never seen in any other instance. It forcibly brought to my mind that beautiful simile in Lord Byron's 'Giaour:'

> " He who hath bent him o'er the dead
> Ere the first day of death has fled;
> Before Decay's effacing fingers
> Have swept the lines where beauty lingers,
> And mark'd the mild angelic air,
> The rapture of repose that's there,
> The fixed yet tender traits that streak
> The languor of the placid cheek—
> * * * * *
> He still might doubt the tyrant's power—
> So fair, so calm, so softly seal'd
> The first, last look, by death reveal'd."

I was one of our deceased friend's executors, and, as my co-executor lived at a considerable distance, the sole direction of her funeral and the settlement of her affairs devolved upon me. These duties, together with the funeral of our son, and the claims of all my other engagements, bore too heavily upon my feeble frame, and in consequence I was soon afterwards seriously ill. My asthmatic disorder came upon me with much force, and I was soon a good deal reduced in regard to strength. I wish to avoid even the semblance of affectation, and therefore will not enlarge upon the feelings produced by the decease of those whom I loved or esteemed. Yet it may, perhaps, be allowable to state, that these bereavements produced much painful emotion. I sometimes fancied that I heard the voices which Death had silenced, or saw the forms that had descended into the grave. Altogether I cannot help thinking that the very disordered state into which I now fell was, in part, the result of pensive recollections; at all events my health, from that time, has been in a very broken and disturbed condition. Throughout the year 1833 I was much afflicted by my asthmatic complaint; the attacks were repeated at intervals of little more than a month, and moreover were very violent—so much so indeed, on several occasions, as to threaten a fatal termination. Their effect upon both my person and my affairs was not a little injurious. Towards the close of the year, when I was slowly recovering from one of these attacks, I was considering what could be done to ward off a heavier disaster than any which had hitherto happened to us. The subject was both painful and complicated; and I knew not what to decide upon. All at once it occurred to me that there was a *possibility* of getting some help by the publication of what I had read before the Literary Society. The impression remaining with me, and growing stronger, I thought it well not to neglect it, —being inclined to regard it as an intimation of what I ought to do. I forthwith consulted the principal members of the Society; who advised me to publish, and promised to assist me in getting subscribers for the book. Their generous exertions herein were far more successful than I could have looked for; I did the best I could to prepare the manuscript for the press; and in the latter part of the summer of 1834 it was published. The subscribers' copies brought enough money to pay the printer's bill, and also to leave me a most useful and timely supply for my family. The copies remaining after the subscribers were served amounted to about six hundred. These, partly by personal exertions, and partly by the help of friends, were gradually sold. The money they produced has *oftentimes* been the means of saving us from painful privations. The sale extended over a period of nearly six years. Here then I saw the utility of having, when young, sought amusement in reading and observation rather than in the foolish or vicious pursuits which, in general, are so eagerly followed by young men of my own class.

But there were other, and still more valuable, benefits which resulted from the publication of my little book. It was reviewed in a good many different journals, and, in each case, with much kindness on the part of the reviewer. Some of these notices did me good service; but none of them was nearly so useful as was one that appeared in a weekly Review, published by an eminent and liberal-minded London bookseller. I valued this the more, because I was an entire stranger both to this gentleman and the writer of the notice in his Review. By their assistance it was that I became known to several kind-hearted gentlemen, who, from that time to the present, have been my generous patrons: to one of them, indeed, I owe a very large debt of gratitude, for many and various favours. I will only add, that nearly all the *tailoring* business I have had for the last eight years has come to me through having published my small volume.

In the beginning of 1835 I had occasion to visit London, and while there was attacked by my implacable enemy—asthma. At the commencement of the attack I was put into considerable danger by one of that reckless class of human beings—the cabmen. I was in the street, and unable to speak more than a word or two, on account of my very difficult respiration. I made signs that I wanted to ride, when the driver of the vehicle I had selected, who, I suppose, judged that I was intoxicated, tumbled me about in a way that was as unsafe as it was unpleasant. I received a heavy blow on one of my legs, but thought myself favoured in getting off without more serious injury. The attack was a severe one, and left me in a sadly enfeebled state: happily I was staying with a most kind-hearted friend, who spared neither trouble nor expense in order to relieve and restore me. About the middle of this year I was invited to read a lecture before a Society in a neighbouring town to which I became known through my recently-published book; I accepted the invitation, and had the pleasure of being both thanked and paid for my services. Subsequently, at the request of a similar Society, I read this lecture a second time. It was afterwards printed, and sold well enough to reward me fairly for all the time and labour I had bestowed upon it.

I am now brought to the year 1836—the last of my residence in the country. My sadly disordered state greatly hindered me in my efforts to earn a living. One of my kind patrons—a physician, who *then* took, as he *still* most kindly takes, a great interest in my well-being, advised me, if possible, to seek relief from a change of air. He assured me that nothing more could be done for me in the way of medicine while I continued to breathe the somewhat keen air of my native town. I therefore resolved to try whether that of London would be more favourable: I had, as I have already observed, been effectually relieved by it when a younger man, and I hoped it might prove useful to me again, although I did not expect it would be so to the same extent as formerly. I was quite sure that the asthmatic attack I encountered in London in 1835, was brought on by the cold and fatigue I endured in my journey thither; and therefore considered it as forming no ground of argument against my making the proposed experiment. My little affairs were forthwith arranged, and, aided by the help of some generous friends, I found my way to London. I came, with my family and household goods, in a covered waggon, which I had hired for our sole use. It was, upon the whole, a comfortable mode of travelling, but required that we should be on the road during the night. This was too much for me, especially as I was a good deal worn by the anxiety and fatigue I had undergone in preparing for our journey. On the day after my arrival in town, I was so fiercely run upon by my old enemy, that I apprehended a fatal issue. After the struggle was over, I was for nearly a fortnight in a state of feebleness that made it impossible for me to be useful to my family. On getting a little stronger I set about doing what I could; I succeeded in getting a few orders for clothes, and also in selling a good many copies of my little books. Thus we procured the means of living, although in a very sparing way.

Still we kept our ground, hoping for better days. In the middle of 1837 I had another violent fit of my old complaint, brought on, as usual, by over-fatigue, in conjunction with a slight cold; this happily proved to be the last of these very severe attacks. The change of air now began to work upon me favourably; and I seconded its operations by leaving off the use of emetic or nauseating medicines, which, while they are useful in checking the violence of an asthmatic paroxysm, are, by their weakening qualities, the means of predisposing the patient for another attack. Thus the great object of my coming to London was attained—as far as I could reasonably look for. I did not, however, recover much, if any thing, of my long-lost strength.

Meanwhile I went on as well as I was able, and was as usual cheerfully assisted, in all possible ways, by my faithful and diligent helpmate. In my leisure-hours during this year, and the years 1838 and 1839, I read the whole of Shakspere's dramatic works, Mr. Sharon Turner's 'Sacred History of the Creation,' the ' Memoirs of Mr. Samuel Drew,' and Dr. Stilling's ' Theory of Pneumatology,' together with some odd volumes of the Edinburgh and Quarterly Reviews.

In 1840 I again earned a seasonable supply of money by the use of my pen. In this instance I worked for the bookseller to whom I have already alluded. I was well satisfied with every part of that gentleman's conduct towards me. In my hours of leisure I read the works of Mr. Charles Lamb, Mr. Holcroft's Memoirs, and the 'Life of General Washington.' About midsummer I began to write this account of my own life. From that time to the present I have not read much. I have, however, looked through Lord Byron's works, the 'Memoirs of Mr. William Hutton,' and Dr. Stilling's Autobiography; with some of the works of Sir Walter Scott, Dr. Southey, and Miss Martineau. Meanwhile I have worked diligently at my proper business, at all times when I have not been seriously ill; but I have often been disabled. When too ill to work, I have been unable to amuse myself with a book, or even a newspaper. At the present time I am much debilitated, while it is pretty certain that I shall gradually become still more feeble. I am, in truth, a prematurely old and worn-out man. All the physical infirmities of advanced age have come upon me before I have got much beyond my fifty-second year. I can do nothing without incurring thereby some additional uneasiness. Thus the pathway of my life is overshadowed by a cloud and strewn with thorns. The health and vigour of the body are gone for ever; yet, so long as I am not bereft of all mental activity and cheerfulness,

"——————————————— I argue not
Against Heaven's hand or will, nor bate a jot
Of heart or hope; but still bear up and steer
Right onward."

By the help of memory and fancy I contrive to beguile many an hour that otherwise would be tedious, or perchance painful. The first brings before me pleasant recollections of bygone times, and enables me again to draw amusement or instruction from what I read in my early years; while the latter either carries me into distant scenes, or invests those around me with new and sometimes beautiful features. Except when wholly overborne by bodily pain or infirmity, I am *rarely* unemployed, either in the daytime or in the sleepless hours of the night, of which I have not a few. I aim to be useful, and am occasionally encouraged to believe that I am not wholly unsuccessful. Not unfrequently a cheering ray breaks through the clouds that rest upon the future, and shows me some glimpses of a brighter world and a happier state of being. Thus I pursue my course with tolerable equanimity of feeling. There is much attainable good wherewith to compensate the inevitable evils of my lot. I aim to secure the first, and would fain extract some good from the second. Unceasing occupation of the mind upon some given subject, and with a view to the happiness of others, is one of the best means of drawing off the attention from personal sufferings, and of preventing the affections from becoming either chilled or selfish. The work of writing these Memoirs has many a time raised me above the depressing influence of great bodily disorder. I should grieve that my task is done, but that I have already resolved to begin another.

THE END.

London: Printed by William Clowes and Sons, Stamford Street.

www.ingramcontent.com/pod-product-compliance
Lightning Source LLC
LaVergne TN
LVHW061213060426
835507LV00016B/1910